T0067901

Six Saints from Allegany

God's Grace During Tragedies

Valgene Dunham

WESTBOW
PRESS®
A DIVISION OF THOMAS NELSON
& ZONDERVAN

All Scripture quotations, unless otherwise indicated, are taken from the Holy Bible, New International Version®, NIV®. Copyright ©1973, 1978, 1984, 2011 by Biblica, Inc.™ Used by permission of Zondervan. All rights reserved worldwide. www.zondervan.com The "NIV" and "New International Version" are trademarks registered in the United States Patent and Trademark Office by Biblica, Inc.™

This book is a work of non-fiction. Unless otherwise noted, the author and the publisher make no explicit guarantees as to the accuracy of the information contained in this book and in some cases, names of people and places have been altered to protect their privacy.

WestBow Press books may be ordered through booksellers or by contacting:

WestBow Press
A Division of Thomas Nelson & Zondervan
1663 Liberty Drive
Bloomington, IN 47403
www.westbowpress.com
1 (866) 928-1240

Because of the dynamic nature of the Internet, any web addresses or links contained in this book may have changed since publication and may no longer be valid. The views expressed in this work are solely those of the author and do not necessarily reflect the views of the publisher, and the publisher hereby disclaims any responsibility for them.

Any people depicted in stock imagery provided by Thinkstock are models, and such images are being used for illustrative purposes only.
Certain stock imagery ©·Thinkstock.

ISBN: 978-1-5127-9672-8 (sc)
ISBN: 978-1-5127-9671-1 (hc)
ISBN: 978-1-5127-9673-5 (e)

Library of Congress Control Number: 2017912264

Print information available on the last page.

WestBow Press rev. date: 9/6/2017

Dedicated to the descendants of the Six Saints from Allegany.

She stood in the storm.
And when the wind did not blow her away,
She adjusted her sails.

Elizabeth Edwards, *Resilience: The New Afterword*,
Random House, 2009

If thou but suffer God to guide thee, and hope in Him through all thy ways, He'll give thee strength, what e'er betide thee, and bear thee thro' the evil days; who trusts in God's unchanging love builds on the rock that naught can move. Georg Neumark, 1661. "If thou but suffer God to guide thee." *Hymns for the Living Church*, Hope Publishing, 1974.

CONTENTS

Everlasting Arms

One evening while surfing TV channels, I stopped on the movie "True Grit." I remained on the channel expecting to see the entire cast of well know actors including, John Wayne, Kim Darby, Robert Duvall, and Dennis Hopper. I soon realized that I was watching the new version (2010) with Jeff Bridges, Matt Damon, Josh Brolin. and Hailee Steinfeld. Near the end of the movie as the credits began, I heard the singing of the old hymn of faith "Leaning on the Everlasting Arms." The simple American mountain style of the singer, Iris Dement, had me quietly singing along. Tears came to my eyes as I remembered a picture that used to hang in the Dunham home: "Underneath are the everlasting arms. Deuteronomy 33:27." I had just self-published a family history for relatives and friends entitled *Echoes from the Empty House on the Corner: Family, Faith, and Tragedy*, so God's care for five generations of relatives was fresh on my mind and heart.

God speaks to me quite often through music and His creation. I am reminded by John Donne, poet and former cleric of the Church of England, that God speaks by diverse means:

> God hath divers ways into divers men. Into some he comes at noon, in the sunshine of prosperity; to some in the dark and heavy clouds of adversity. Some he affects with the music of the church; some, with some particular collect or prayer; some, with

some passage of a sermon, which takes no hold of him that stands next to him. Watch the ways the Spirit of God [comes] into thee.[1]

This devotional book has resulted from a re-focus on God's "everlasting arms" that have undergirded selected individuals from my family history. I have selected six women: Mary Eliza Trowbridge Whitlock (1831-1889, my great, great grandmother); Ellen Jane Linderman Whitlock (1884-1962, my grandaunt); Grace Olivia Whitney Whitlock (1890-1970, my grandmother); and her three daughters: Viola Fern Whitlock Dunham (1914-2005, my mother); Alma Maud Whitlock Chesebro Rex (1917-2008, my aunt); and Medora Whitlock Potter (1922-1961, my aunt). This collection is non-fictional and documented. Each one of these saints of God experienced God's blessings during their lives as well as the "everlasting arms" of their Lord and Savior, Jesus Christ, during tragedy and loss.

May the words of this book, whether my own or taken from hymns, the scriptures, famous quotes, or from the diaries and essays of relatives, provide one of the "divers" ways by which God will speak to you.

> Psalm 71:17, 18 Since my youth, O God, you have taught me, and to this day I declare your marvelous deeds. Even when I am old and gray, do not forsake me, O God, till I declare your power to the next generation, your might to all who are to come.

> Psalm 145:3-7 Great is the Lord and most worthy of praise; his greatness no one can fathom. **One generation will commend your works to another**; **they** will tell of your mighty acts. **They** will speak of the glorious splendor of your majesty, and **I** will meditate on your wonderful works. **They** will tell of the power of your awesome works, and **I** will proclaim your great deeds. **They** will celebrate your abundant goodness and joyfully sing of your righteousness.

Acknowledgements

Every family group requires a "collector;" a person who is willing to collect documents, and photographs, and, most importantly, be willing to seek such memoranda. The extended Whitlock/Whitney family, a focus of this devotional, has such a collector: Howard Mark Whitney. Mark not only found and saved the letters of our great, great grandfather, William Whitlock, before he was killed in the Civil War, but also has continued to make collections from the succeeding generations. Other relatives, such as the Chesebros, Potters, and my siblings, have contributed written remembrances and photos.

I appreciate the assistance of the staff of WestBow Press, starting with Phil Yeager, who convinced me of publishing with WestBow. Hannah Ermac and Reggie Adams were very helpful in directing me in the submission of the manuscript.

Most importantly, I thank God for bringing all of the people named in this devotional into my life through research involved in producing this book.

Valgene Dunham
Conway, South Carolina
July, 2107

1

The Place

John 1:1-3. In the beginning was the Word, and the Word was with God, and the Word was God. He was with God in the beginning. Through him all things were made... In him was life, and that life was the light of men.

As a scientist (asking mechanistic questions) and as a Christian (asking faith-based questions), I am encouraged to see the long opposition between science and the scriptures continue to dissolve. This coming together over the understanding of beginnings is exciting to me in that I see the Big Bang as God the Father saying "Let it happen"!

The recent discovery of gravitational waves, predicted by Einstein and expected in the Big Bang, reminds me of a number of Biblical verses describing the creation as God "stretching out his hand" in the expansion of the universe.[1] I see nothing in the theory that eliminates an all powerful, all knowing God, employing his Son, Jesus Christ, as the necessary power to make it happen and to hold it together. Consequently, I can ask questions of origin while my faith answers the "Why" question: All for the honor and glory of God and his Son, Jesus Christ. C. S. Lewis indicates that if one is looking for God, they can find him. "Send a saint up in a spaceship and he'll find God in space as he found God on earth. Much depends on the seeing eye."[2]

"Lord of life, beneath the dome of the universe, thy home,
Gather us who seek thy face to the fold of thy embrace for thou art nigh.
Holy, Holy, Holy, Lord God of Hosts! Heav'n and earth are full of Thee!
Heav'n and earth are praising thee, O Lord most high!"[3]

"The spacious firmament on high, with all the blue ethereal sky,
And spangled heav'ns, a shining frame, their great Original proclaim.
Th'unwearied sun, from day to day, does his Creator's pow'r display;
And publishes to every land the work of an almighty hand."[4]

Deuteronomy 4:35, 39 You were shown these things so that you might know that the Lord is God; besides him there is no other. Acknowledge and take to heart this day that the Lord is God in heaven above and on the earth below. There is no other.

The characteristics of God, especially omnipotence, omniscience and omnipresence, lead me to believe that conditions and characteristics of the earth's surface, created by Him over time as described above, were known by God to suit the desires, wishes, education and training, and careers of individuals and families in the future. After all, He prepared the Garden of Eden and is presently preparing a place for us. I present to you in this non-fictional devotional book, a certain locale in the United States that suited the William Whitlock family; where they would come to know and worship God, serve their neighbors, and become all that God intended them to be. The Five Mile Valley, in southern Cattaraugus County, of western New York State is that place. He didn't promise a rose garden, but he did promise the support of his "everlasting arms."

"Under the protecting shadow of God's wing the little shadows of life lose their terror."[5]

2

The Valley

The Five Mile Valley, Allegany, New York. Photography by author, 2009.

If the wooded hills of western New York could speak, they would tell how they were formed over millions of years by seas and glaciers. They would speak to the special forces that made Cattaraugus County unique in that it was not entirely covered by the glaciers that shaped the land of other counties in New York. In fact, this area of western New York was the only area this far north in the eastern United States not molded by advancing glaciers during the Ice Age. Within the county are three physiographic provinces:

1. Erie-Ontario Plain--lowland making up only five percent of the county, located in the northwest corner bordered by Cattaraugus Creek.
2. Allegheny Plateau--glaciated area making up seventy-five percent of the county; characterized by steep valley walls with wide ridge tops and flat-topped hills.
3. Allegheny Plateau--unglaciated area making up twenty percent of the southern county along the Allegheny River. This area of New York, the Salamanca Re-entrant, is the most northern region of unglaciated land in eastern North America. The area, located in southern Cattaraugus County in the USGS Knapp Creek Topographic Quadrangle, has long steep slopes and a maximum recorded elevation of 2,430 feet, in the town of Allegany. The plateau is an extension of the Allegheny Plateau from nearby Pennsylvania. Therefore, southern Cattaraugus County is part of the same oil fields found in northwest Pennsylvania.[1]

The bedrock under this "special" section are primarily sandstone, siltstone or sandstone conglomerate. There are two major soil groups formed from these weathered rock types along the Allegheny River near the town of Allegany.[2]

1. Chenango-Pawling-Holderton series found on the floor of valleys such as the Five Mile Valley
2. Volusia-Mardin series found on the slopes of most of the valleys[3]

These soil types were developed over years of soil formation carried out by factors such as the parent bedrock, relief (slope of the land in relation to the water table), climate, plant and animal life, and time. In general, sandy or gravelly loam soils, such as Chenango, Castile, Valois and Holderton (if drained) on flat or slightly sloped land, are all found specifically in the Allegany area of Cattaraugus County and provide excellent farm lands.[4]

One of the most picturesque places in all of western New York is the Five Mile Valley seen from Chapel Hill, a steep hill that separates the valley from Humphrey, New York. From the hill, one can see the house that originally was the Five Mile Baptist Church, where numerous members of the extended Whitlock family gathered to worship. Nearby is the Five Mile Cemetery, where they rest. The farmhouse, in which four of the six Whitlock women that serve as the focus of this book lived, has deteriorated but is still standing.

Whitlock/Whitney Farmhouse, Photography by author, 2014

Meandering through this former area of dairy farms is the Five Mile Creek that flows south toward the Town of Allegany where the creek meets the Allegheny River. The river has provided a significant advantage to the area and originates near Raymond (Potter County), in north central Pennsylvania. It flows into western New York for approximately 30 miles, before returning to Pennsylvania, where it joins the Monongahela River in Pittsburgh to form the Ohio River. Consequently, the forces of climate change and the movement of water created a special valley, the products of which could be transported to other regions. These included lumber and wood products, tanned hides, dairy products and oil.[5] Therefore, the land in and around the Five Mile Valley allowed for the immigration of the Whitlock family into an opportunity for sustained farming and continued employment.

3

The Pilgrimage

Genesis 12:1 Leave your country, your people and your father's household and go to the land I will show you.

John Whitlock, one of three sons of Reuben and Christina Whitlock of Monmouth, New Jersey, heard the call of central New York. After his marriage to Mary Morris on December 26, 1793, John and Mary moved to a town at the tip of one of the Finger Lakes, Cayuga Lake, an area that would be named Tompkins County in 1817.[1] Records indicate that the couple had five children when they moved, including twin boys, Thomas and Morris, who were born April 24, 1801 in New Jersey.[2] This move was quite adventuresome since the area was under the control of the Saponi and Tutelo, tribes of the Cayuga Indians, as late as 1789.[3]

Perhaps because of the reputation of the frontier town of Ithaca, New York, at the time, (Sin City, Sodom), John and Mary were concerned about raising their large family in a Christian atmosphere. They had added seven more children after moving from New Jersey. They and their 13 children jointed the First Presbyterian Church in Ithaca on June 9, 1816.[4]

For the Whitlock family, involved in farming and lumbering, this area of western New York held quite a number of advantages. The quality and diversity of the vegetation included a variety of maples, with the sugar maple conspicuous, and oaks of several species. Thomas, one of John and

Mary's twin boys, and one of his sons, William, both married women from Rice, NY (later named Ischua, in 1855). At the age of 19, (1820), Thomas married Jane Norton who was two years younger. Between 1830 and 1835, Thomas moved his wife and their six children to Ischua, Jane's hometown. Not only was the town the birthplace of Jane and the location of her family, it was significantly far enough away from the activity and reputation of Ithaca. More importantly, the rapidly depleted forests of Tompkins County may have pointed the family to the less developed area around Ischua.[5]

In a poem "Travelling," by Frank Topping, the author indicates that God travels with us no matter where we go and includes a prayer for guidance, peace, and uniting with loved ones.[6] The uniting with relatives has always been an important factor in determining the location of a settlement.

William Whitlock was a shingle maker and farmer. He was born on May 3, 1829 in Tompkins County, New York, the sixth child of Thomas and Jane Norton Whitlock[7] By the 1850 census, at age 21, William was listed as living in Ischua, had moved out of his parents home, and was employed working with wood as a shingle maker. Two other families were also on pilgrimage to the Five Mile Valley. Dr. James and Olive Sackett Trowbridge brought their ten children to the area where James became one of the first physicians to set up a practice in the Allegany area.[8] Another prominent family that moved from Ithaca to the Five Mile Valley was the Lindermans. The Lindermans, Whitlocks and the Trowbridges intermarried while the families lived in Ithaca.

Through God's overseeing guidance, these three families were now within two miles of each other's farms. One of the major reasons for people in pilgrimage to settle in the same area is religion.[9] The church was often the center of the community at which the worship of God helped to bring people together and form solid, cooperative communities. One of the more important aspects of the church's role was to bring young people together in a social context in which future marriage partners came to love each other.

Psalms 84:5-7. "Blessed are those whose strength is in you, who have set their hearts on pilgrimage. As they pass through the Five Mile Valley (inserted by author), they make it a place of springs; the autumn rains also cover it with pools. They go from strength to strength, till each appears before God in Zion."

4

Saints, Sinners, Savior

John Wesley Hipp, pastor at the First Methodist Church, Conway, South Carolina, from 2001 to 2003, before being called to return to serve as chaplain in the Armed Services, started each sermon with a greeting: "Good Morning Saints." The congregation would respond, "Good Morning!" Rev. Hipp then followed with "Good Morning Sinners." The people would respond, "Good Morning," perhaps not as loudly or with the same enthusiasm. Rev. Hipp was reminding us that the difference between saints and sinners is the Savior, Jesus Christ and how we allow his teachings to guide us in our walk with God.

John Calvin, much earlier in 1536, in *Institutes of the Christian Religion*, pointed out the relationship between sinner, saint, and savior in an essay on "The Believer's Acceptance in Jesus Christ."

We confess that it is Jesus Christ who is given to us by the Father, in order that in Him we should recover all of which in ourselves we are deficient.

1. Being in our own nature enemies of God and subject to His wrath and judgment, we are reconciled with Him and received again in grace through the intercession of Jesus Christ

2. We acknowledge that by His spirit we are regenerated into a new spiritual nature. The evils of our flesh are mortified by grace, so that they rule us no longer.

3. We acknowledge that this regeneration is so effected in us that, until we slough off this mortal body, there remains always in us much imperfection and infirmity.[1]

So what is a saint? Numerous dictionary definitions include a saint to be a holy or virtuous person whose attributes include kindness, righteousness, and patience. This devotional book is based on the definition of saint as used by the Apostle Paul in his letters to the churches in the New Testament. The word used in the New Testament for saint is the Hebrew word "hagios," which means sacred or holy thing. The Hebrew word in the Old Testament is "chaciyd," translated faithful, kind, godly, and holy one. Another word for saint is "qadowsh," meaning set apart, sacred, and holy.[2] It would appear that to be a saint, one must be righteous, virtuous, kind, and holy. It is immediately clear that these qualifications eliminate all of us. When listing the attributes of saints: endurance, obedience, humility, patience and faith, it would seem impossible to possess these characteristics while alive here on earth. Through the grace of God, humans can be saints after accepting Christ as Savior and Lord. Saints are not perfect individuals but are people who are continually seeking God's will for their lives and showing His love to others. Paul refers to these people in the plural, perhaps indicating that importance of the church to these early Christians.

> "Love divine, all loves excelling, Joy of heav'n, to earth come down;
> Fix in us Thy humble dwelling, All Thy faithful mercies crown.
> Jesus, Thou art all compassion, Pure, unbounded love Thou art;
> Visit us with Thy salvation; Enter every trembling heart.
> Finish then Thy new creation, Pure and spotless let us be;
> Let us see Thy great salvation Perfectly restored in Thee;
> Changed from glory into glory, Till in heav'n we take our place,
> Till we cast our crowns before Thee, Lost in wonder, love and praise."[3]

This hymn should be the prayer of every Christian: to allow God to fix in our hearts a dwelling for God's Holy Spirit to guide our humble service to others.

I am amazed at the diversity of people who God chooses and develops as His followers and saints. He has chosen people who were held in high regard by their communities because of their education (Saul, a Pharisee from Tarsus, Turkey; Luke, a doctor from Antioch, Syria) or their moral standing (Joseph of Nazareth); those held in low regard because of their employment as tax collectors (Matthew of Capernaum and Zacchaeus from Jericho). God's love was even displayed through a group in low standing in the culture: females.

Early followers of Jesus Christ included many women. Mary, the mother of Jesus, lived in Nazareth and followed Christ during his ministry and was present at the crucifixion. She was a member of the early Christian community in Jerusalem. Other women important in the support of the apostles and to the early Christian church came from diverse backgrounds.

Joanna, the wife of Chuza, the steward to Herod the Tetrach, was healed by Jesus, and followed him and supported his ministry with her own wealth. She was at the cross and the empty tomb. Luke 8:1-3; 23:55; 24:10.

Junia was an apostle and highly regarded by Paul, "a patron of many Christian." Romans 16:1, 2

Lydia, Chloe and Nympha were house church leaders: Lydia was a seller of purple cloth in Thyatira and worshipped God. When she heard the gospel from Paul, she and her household became Christians. Chloe was emblematic of fruitful grace and beauty and provided lodging for Paul in Corinth. Nympha, a woman of means in Corinth, provided a room or house large enough to hold the growing new Christian church. Acts 16:14, 15; I Corinthians 1:19, 11; Colossians 4:15.

Mary Magdalene was from Magdala, a wicked town on the coast of Galilee. Jesus expelled seven demons from her. She was a faithful follower and supporter of Jesus during his ministry. Mark 5:40, 47; 16:1-19; John 19:25; 20:1-18.

Mary and Martha of Bethany were visited by Jesus four times. Luke 10:38-42.

Mary, the mother of James, followed Jesus and used her own resources to assist his ministry. She was at the cross and carried spices to the empty tomb. Matthew 27:55.

Phoebe was a deacon and leader in the church at Cenchreae. She was trusted by Paul to deliver his letter to the Romans. She opened her house to Paul and other Christians. Romans 16:1, 2.

Tryphena and Tryphosa were Greek women of noble birth who lived in luxury. Paul said that they "worked hard for the Lord." Romans 16:12.

Priscilla was from a distinguished Roman family and was married to Aquila (a Jew). They left Rome when Claudius forced all the Jews to leave. They met Paul in Corinth and he lived with them for 18 months. She was a tentmaker like Paul and firmly established in the faith. When Paul left Corinth, Priscilla and Aquila went with him to Ephesus, where they were able to minister to Apollos. Acts 18:2, 18, 26.

Through my research and personal acquaintance of four of the six individuals discussed in this book, I invite you to join me in thanking God for the attributes of saints that these imperfect ladies from the farms of western New York exhibited to their friends, families, and their descendants.

5

Mary Eliza Trowbridge Whitlock

Mary Eliza Trowbridge was born in Hinsdale, New York, to the parents of one of the first physicians in the Allegany area of western New York.[1] Mary Eliza Trowbridge Whitlock was a special lady whom William Whitlock, her husband, called "Liddy" and phonetically spelled "Lide". Lide, born on October 30, 1831, was the eighth of ten children parented by Dr. James and Olive Sackett Trowbridge. The Whitlock and Trowbridge families had been neighbors in the area of Ischua, Hinsdale, Humphrey, and Allegany, New York. On September 9, 1850, William Whitlock was married to Mary Eliza Trowbridge in a double ring ceremony in Humphrey, New York, just over Chapel Hill from the Five Mile Valley.[2] A lumberman/farmer had married a daughter of a physician. Lide brought the need for education of children to the marriage as evidenced by Will's letters (see below). They were attracted to each other and held together by a mutual love of God, the church community, and the availability of family for assistance when needed.

> Ephesians 2:19, 20. You are no longer foreigners and aliens, but fellow citizens with God's people and members of God's household, built on the foundation...with Christ Jesus himself as the chief cornerstone.

Mary Eliza Trowbridge Whitlock. c1886. Whitney
Collection. Courtesy of Howard Mark Whitney.

Will and Lide began farming in Humphrey, New York and Will continued to work as a shingle maker like his father and several of his Trowbridge relatives. Farm life on the Allegany frontier was difficult, but Will and Lide trusted in God and relied on their own hard work with assistance from members of their families and others in the community.

> Psalms 24: 5, 6. [They] received blessing from the Lord and vindication from God their Savior. Such is the generation of those who seek him, who seek thy face, O God of Jacob.

Before they moved from Ischua, God blessed this couple with two children: a daughter, Francis Euzetta Whitlock on July 18, 1851, and a son, Stanley Meade Whitlock on December 13, 1853. After moving to Allegany, New York, another daughter was born, Clara Hulda Whitlock on August 10, 1856, and a son, Henry C. Whitlock on July 6, 1860.[3]

By 1850, most citizens realized that the states within the Union, not yet 100 years old, had serious problems. If these problems, high tariffs for southern cotton, industrialization of the north, and slavery, were not successfully negotiated, the country might be in civil war. After the failure of the Great Compromise in 1850, the divided country prepared to go to war. Governor Gist asked other southern governors to join South Carolina in considering secession. On December 18, 1860, the secession convention in Charleston voted secession. Five other deep southern states joined South Carolina. Delegates to the convention remain heroes in South Carolina to the present time.[4]

On April 16, 1861, the New York legislature authorized the governor of New York, Edwin C. Morgan, to call up 13, 280 officers and men from the state in response from a call to arms from the president, Abraham Lincoln. Based on existing letters written by Will, I am sure that he and Lide thought and prayed about Will's involvement in the Civil War.[5] Their children were then ten, eight, five, and one years of age. If Will went to war, how would Lide, with four small children, manage the farm? Will and Lide made the decision for Will to remain on the farm and Will did not enlist after several calls from President Lincoln. After the battle at Gettysburg on July 1-3, 1963, Will and Lide heard about a family in nearby Portville, New York. Sergeant Amos Humiston had left his wife Philinda and three children to join Company C of the New York 154th ("Hardtack Regiment"). Sergeant Humiston was killed during the Battle of Gettysburg on the first day. Dr. John Bourns of Philadelphia, Pennsylvania, who was assisting wounded soldiers and the collection of the deceased, found the body of the unidentified soldier holding an ambrotype of three children in his hand. Philinda saw a written description of the children and their clothing and wondered if she had lost her husband. Four months later she finally saw the picture and knew that her husband had been killed at Gettysburg.[6] The Humiston story may have influenced Will and Lide in making any enlistment decision. By the summer of 1864 and another call for enlistments, Will and Lide may have thought that their children were older now, (Euzetta, Stanley, Clara and Henry were now 13, 11, 8 and 4 years old, respectively) and able to be of assistance to Lide in holding the farm together. With the expected assistance of other family members, including the Trowbridges, Will may have thought it was his time to support his country, and on September 7, 1864, he enlisted at

Allegany, New York, and was mustered into Company A, of the 188th New York Volunteers at Dunkirk, New York, on September 26.[7]

> Psalms 119:105, 109, 111, 112. Your word is a lamp to my feet and a light for my path. Though I constantly take my life in my hands, I will not forget your law. Your statutes are my heritage forever; they are the joy of my heart. My heart is set on keeping your decrees to the very end.

> Luke 1: 78, 79....Because of the tender mercy of our God, by which the rising sun will come to us from heaven to shine on those living in darkness and in the shadow of death, to guide our feet into the path of peace.

Thirty-nine letters of Will to Lide during the Civil War were found in the attic of the Whitlock/Whitney house in the Five Mile Valley. Unfortunately, none of Lide's letters to Will have survived. Her concerns and questions can, however, be seen in his return letters.

Lide infused into her descendants a love and need for education. So much so, that Will expressed concern in his letters of their four children's progress in school. In some of his letters home, Will implies that his writing and his speech were not what he wished them to be in the light of Lide's abilities. This was true especially when Will wrote concerning church membership and his ability to speak in public. Lide brought to the family the need for education through which they could improve their lives by providing opportunities. Lide knew God's warnings about the lack of knowledge in general and, specifically, knowledge of God's laws.

> Hosea 4:6 My people are destroyed for lack of knowledge; because thou hast rejected knowledge, I will also reject thee, that thou shalt be no priest to me, seeing thou has forgotten the law of thy God, I will also forget thy children.

> Proverbs 18:15 The mind of the prudent acquires knowledge, and the ear of the wise seeks knowledge.

Being a military wife was difficult because Lide had to parent alone while feeling alone herself; talking about death, dying and the traumatic effects of war, while choosing happiness in the midst of challenging circumstances, and depending on relatives and friends. On February 3, 1865, Will wrote Lide from camp to the southwest of Petersburg, Virginia, that there were rumors of having to go to a second battle near Hatcher's Run. His children and their education were on his mind. "if you stay there where you are I hope it will be so you can send zitta (Euzetta) to school to Olean next spring, she tells me that she has got over half way through her Arithmatic. I think she has done well. how does Stanley get along with his studys? does Clary (Clara) and Hankey (Henry) learn very fast? tel Hankey pa will have to anssur his letter as soon as he gets a little time. Write often, my love to all. no more so good by."[8]

Three days later in the cool afternoon of February 6, 1965, at the battle of Hatcher's Run II, William Whitlock was killed in the Virginia woods by a Confederate mini ball to the head. His comrades were able to retrieve and bury his body behind their lines. This enabled his friends to prepare a head board to mark the grave. His body was later transferred to nearby Poplar Grove National Cemetery, grave # 2702. It is not known how and when Lide received the news. The Whitlocks and the Trowbridges and other friends must have immediately come to the aid of Lide and her family.[9]

"Under His wings, what a refuge in sorrow!
How the heart yearningly turns to His rest!
Often when earth has no balm for my healing,
There I find comfort and there I am blest.
Under His Wings, under His wings,
Who from His love can sever?
Under His wings my soul shall abide,
Safely abide forever."[10]

"It is the wind of God that dries my vain, regretful tears,
Until with braver thoughts shall rise the purer, brighter years;
If cast on shores of selfish ease or pleasure I should be,
Lord, let me feel thy freshening breeze, and I'll put back to sea."[11]

All of a sudden her oldest son, Stanley Maud Whitlock, became the man of the house. Stanley proved to be a man of God and helped found the Five Mile Baptist Church, where all of the Whitlocks worshiped God. He assisted in the incorporation and registration of the Five Mile Cemetery where they rest.

Five Mile Baptist Church, Church Road, Allegany,
New York. Dunham Collection.

In death's dark vale I fear no ill with Thee, dear Lord, beside me;
Thy rod and staff my comfort still, Thy cross before to guide me.
And so through all the length of days Thy goodness faileth never;
Good Shepherd, may I sing Thy praise within Thy house forever.[12]

My great, great, grandmother, Mary Eliza Trowbridge Whitlock, was a woman of God who suffered through the tragedy of the loss of her husband in battle, and raised her family to honor and glorify the Lord in their lives. Lide died in 1889 and is buried in the Five Mile Cemetery, which her son helped to organize.

6

Ellen Jane Linderman Whitlock

O God, our help in ages past, Our hope for years to come,
Be Thou our guide while life shall last, And our eternal home![1]

My grandaunt, Ellen Linderman, was the youngest of seven children parented by Orson Linderman and Hannah Farwell. The Linderman family had lived near the Whitlocks and Trowbridges in Ischua, Hinsdale, and Humphrey, New York.[2]

Following the death of his father in battle, Will found himself as head of the household at age 12. With the teaching of his mother and the assistance of relatives and neighbors, Stanley matured as a hard-working, God-fearing man. Stanley developed into one of the leading Christian gentlemen in the Five Mile Valley.

In 1877, at the age of 24, Stanley married Medora Linderman (age 18, granddaughter of Nicolas Linderman) and two years later settled in Humphrey to build a eighty-four acre farm. The couple worked strenuously on the farm and took excellent care of Mary Eliza Whitlock, Stanley's mother. Stanley became quite skilled in the management of the farm and employed relatives and neighbors for assistance. They became active in the community which included supporting and joining the local church, at the encouragement of his mother. In 1882, five years after their marriage, the couple was blessed with their first of three children, Ray John Whitlock. Eight years later in 1890, the couple had a second boy, Clare Earl Whitlock. By the time that their third child, Bessie Arlene

Whitlock (1893-1970) was born, the Stanley Whitlock family was well respected in the community. Stanley was active in church and town government and served as the town assessor. As evidenced by their later lives, the three Whitlock children learned from their parents the value of hard work, a love of family, and a strong belief in God.[3]

Another major event in the life of Stanley Whitlock's family occurred in 1897 when he moved his family over Chapel Hill to the Five Mile Valley and Elmwood Farm, owned by John Phillips, at the corner of Five Mile Road and Morgan Hollow Road.[4] This move in location placed the Whitlock farm next door to the farm of Orson and Hannah Farwell Linderman on Five Mile Road. Their youngest daughter, Ellen Jane Linderman, was born in 1884. When the Whitlocks moved in next door to the Lindermans, Ellen was 13 years old, just two years younger than Ray Whitlock. Both sets of parents loved God and supported education by being on the board for School District #5.[5]

The two teenagers got to know each other through school and church activities, fell in love, were married, and began farming across the Five Mile Creek on the West Five Mile Road.

Ellen Jane Linderman Whitlock, Ray John Whitlock. Whitney Collection. Courtesy of Howard Mark Whitney.

Based on Ray's younger brother's diaries (Clare Earl Whitlock), the two Whitlock families were very close, both in the community and at church. God was the center of the home and when he blessed them with children, they were raised to love God and encouraged to make decisions to accept Jesus Christ into their lives as Savior and Lord. Ellen learned to have a heart for witnessing for Christ through missions. By her actions, she exhibited this love to her children.

> Matthew 5:16 Let your light shine before men, that they may see your good deeds and praise your Father in heaven.

God blessed Ray and Ellen with five children: Paul John (1909-1945), Mable Elizabeth (1911-2001), Dana S. (1917-1927), Lenna Jane (1920-1983) and Stanley Meade (1923- 1985).[8]

> "The flower of youth never appears more beautiful than when it bends toward the Son of Righteousness."[6]

Each of Ellen's children served God in a life of service, including missions. Paul was a missionary to Africa, Mable served as the wife of a minister (Rev. Carl Hoeldtke), Lenna taught in a Christian school, and Stanley was a missionary in Tongo (Pacific Ocean) after a career in the Air Force during World War II.[7]

> Proverbs 22:6 Start children off on the way they should go, and even when they are old they will not turn from it.

> Matthew 28:19, 20. Go and make disciples of all nations, baptizing them in the name of the Father, and of the Son and of the Holy Spirit, and teaching them to obey everything I have commanded you. And surely I am with you always, to the very end of the age.

Ellen had a mission. Jesus' disciples were to make disciples and Ellen started at home by wanting her children to be disciples of Christ. "The verb to disciple describes the process by which we encourage another person to be such a follower of Jesus and the means we use to help that person to grow up in Christ."[8] Consequently, Christian parents should be guides by disciplining (what's right and wrong) and guides to discipleship (exhibiting and teaching God's love and grace). Ellen trusted in the promise from Matthew 28; the "everlasting arms" will be with disciples to the end of the age.

About the time that her oldest son, Paul, graduated from Westbrook Commercial Academy in Olean, New York (1927), the clouds of death and tragedy descended on Ellen. One of the life's questions that we often ask is "Why do bad things happen to good people?" Perhaps Ellen was asking that question as the family lowered her child, Dana, into the grave at age 10.[9] Ellen, Ray and their surviving children turned to the "everlasting arms" of God for comfort and support.

> 2 Corinthians 1:3, 4. Praise be to the God and Father of our Lord Jesus Christ, the Father of compassion and the God of all comfort, who comforts us in all our troubles, so that we can comfort those in any trouble with the comfort we ourselves have received from God.

> "Tenderly…may God heal your sorrow.

> Gently…may the prayer of friends ease your hurting.

> Softly…may God's peace replace your heartache with warm, loving memories."[10]

> Isaiah 40:11 He tends His flock like a shepherd: He gathers the lambs in His arms and carries them close to His heart. He gently leads those that have young.

Please notice the adverbs from the above poem and scripture: tenderly, gently, and softly. It is well documented in the diaries of several of the Whitlocks that comforting others brings comfort in return.[11]

I am sure that Ray and Ellen's parents, Stanley and Medora Whitlock and Orson and Hannah Linderman, assisted the grieving family. This coming together of families is a function of the pilgrimage to a given location and a love of God's church. As often the case in frontier history, this church (The Five Mile Baptist Church) was founded with the assistance of a member of the family (Stanley Whitlock). Our hindsight is often an illumination of God's foresight.

Ellen was now specifically praying for Paul and his family who were home on furlough as missionaries to Africa. Ellen was also seeking God's care for Stanley who was in flight training in the Air Force, all in the context of World War II (1943). While working and studying in Philadelphia, Paul had married Helen Magnin, a daughter of a missionary to Africa. They served a six and a half year term, and were now planning to return to Africa with their family of five sons, Paul John, Jr., Kenneth E., Robert Allen, Richard Thomas, and Stanley Magnin. Ellen's brother-in-law, Clare Whitlock, was admitted to the Olean General Hospital on Tuesday, May 25, 1943. He was suffering from heart disease and the family was greatly concerned that Clare might never return home.

Three days later on Friday, May 28, 1943, tragedy struck the Whitlock brothers, but not Clare. It was Ellen's husband Ray. At 2 A.M., Ellen called her sister-in-law, Grace Whitlock, and told her that Ray had suddenly died of a heart attack. Clare's condition was so severe that the family never told him of Ray's passing. Clare died on July 7th in Saint Francis Hospital in Olean, New York.[12]

In a span of two months, Ellen had lost her husband and brother-in-law. The sudden loss of a husband is usually devastating and no different for a Christian woman like Ellen. After all, she had already lost a child. Sabrina Beasley McDonald, in an article written after losing her young husband in an automobile accident, tells that her "soul bled profusely like a severed limb", and she "needed a tourniquet to stop the bleeding." She found that "many wonderful books about grief, heaven, and peace, were helpful but did not address the wound. To address the wound in her heart, she realized that she needed to go back to the Bible so that God could help her renew her mind.[13]

> Romans 12:2 Do not conform any longer to the pattern of this world, but be transformed by the renewing of your mind. Then

you will be able to test and approve what God's will is—his good, pleasing and perfect will.

Ellen's oldest son, Paul, and his family, are now ready to return to Tanzania (1945). After placing the two eldest boys in boarding school in Florida, Paul, Helen and the three youngest boys boarded the <u>China Clipper</u> for Africa on January 7th.

At about 9:00 PM on January 8, 1945, while landing at Port of Spain, Trinidad, tragedy struck when the *Clipper* crashed into the water at an incorrect angle when flying too rapidly, apparently due to pilot error. All of the Whitlocks on board were killed.[14]

Suddenly, Ellen Jane Linderman Whitlock, who lost one of her children at an early age (Dana), her husband, and her brother-in-law just two years before the crash, was faced with the loss of her oldest son, her daughter-in-law and three grandsons. Committal services for 13 of the crash victims (including the Whitlocks) were held at the Port of Spain Cemetery on January 11, 1945 by chaplains, with Pan American Airlines staff in attendance.[15] As a boy of four and one half years of age, I did not understand the full implications of the crash. I do remember the sorrow in my mother's eyes. Because of the love of family and Christian missions, the death of Ellen's son Paul and most of his family, reverberated through the entire Five Mile Valley.

Ellen immediately turned to God and her other children for comfort and support and went to Chicago to live with Lenna, her oldest daughter, and was there to see Lenna graduate from Moody Bible Institute. Ellen and Lenna moved to Philadelphia, where Lenna became a school teacher at the Northeast Christian Day School.[16]

Ellen Jane Linderman Whitlock, a woman of strong faith, tested repeatedly in the face of tragedies, died in Philadelphia in 1962, and is buried back home in Allegany Cemetery, Section S3, Plot18, Grave 2. Her supportive daughter, Lenna, moved to Florida in retirement.[17]

> "If thou but suffer God to guide thee, And hope in Him through all thy ways,

He'll give thee strength, what e'er betide thee, And bear thee thro' the evil days;

Who trusts in God's unchanging love Builds on the rock that naught can move."[18]

7

Grace Olivia Whitney Whitlock

In hind sight, J. Warner and Arvilla Whitney chose the perfect name for their youngest daughter: Grace. One of eight children, Grace exhibited goodness and generosity throughout her life and exemplified "God's favor."

In Acts 11, we are told of the spreading of the news of Stephen's martyrdom in Antioch and that even Gentiles believed in Jesus Christ. When the news reached the church at Jerusalem, they sent Barnabas to check things out.

> Acts 11:23 When he arrived and saw the evidence of the grace of God, he was glad and encouraged them all to remain true to the Lord with all their hearts.

That is exactly what people saw when they knew the life and testimony of Grace Olivia Whitney.

Another family that settled in Humphrey, New York, in addition to the Whitlocks, Lindermans and Trowbridges, was a number of Whitney family groups. Grace Olivia Whitney, was born in Humphrey on March 27, 1891. One of eight children, she had four older brothers who were all born in Kansas where her father, J. Warner Whitney, had moved to teach and farm. Upon returning to Humphrey and settling on Howe Hill, the couple had three girls: Ethel, Mae, Grace and a son, Howard. J.

Warner and Arvilla taught their children the love of God and the need of a personal savior.[1] All of the children grew up to be fine Christians and contributed greatly to their communities.

The shy, soft-spoken, Grace became acquainted with Clare and Bessie Whitlock, (about the same age as Grace), through attendance at the Baptist church and grammar school in Humphrey. In 1897, the Stanley Whitlock family moved to the Five Mile.[2] It is certain that Clare Whitlock and Grace Whitney, in the small village atmosphere in Humphrey and along the Five Mile Road, saw each other at social gatherings and got to know and love each other.

On November 13, 1912, they were married.[3] Clare (age 22) had developed a strong work ethic and was an important member of the developing farm and of the Five Mile Baptist Church, founded by his father. Both Clare's work ethic, intelligence, and his Christianity attracted the farmer's daughter, Grace Whitney (age 21).

Grace was now thrust into the center of farm activity and development at the corner of Five Mile and Morgan Hollow Roads. In this area along the Five Mile Road, large active dairy farms were growing rapidly under the ownership of the Whitlocks and Lindermans. Any social activity that Grace participated in before her marriage certainly served her well in this new environment. When Grace moved into the brick house as Clare's wife, Clare had lived in the house since he was seven years old. Stanley and Medora Linderman Whitlock, Clare's parents, were still living there as well. Grace lived with her parents-in-law for five years until Stanley and Medora Whitlock moved to Allegany in 1917.[4] With two very dominate male figures in her life, her husband and father-in-law, this shy young woman put to use the grace she received from the Lord with the social skills she had learned growing up in a large family. Also during this time, Grace gave birth to her first daughter, Viola Fern Whitlock, on March 16, 1914 (Chapter 8).[5] When Stanley and Medora moved to Allegany three years later, Grace's parents, Joseph Warner Whitney and Arvilla Fuller Whitney, took their place in the red brick house on the corner. Her parents were welcomed into the house in the same year that Grace almost died having her second child, Alma Maud Whitlock, on February 9, 1917 (Chapter 9).[6] One year after her father died in 1922,

Grace experienced another near death experience by bringing into the world her third daughter, Medora Arvilla Whitlock (Chapter 10).[7] While still recuperating, another very important change occurred with respect to the residents and owners of the house. Howard Whitney (Grace's younger brother) had married Bessie Whitlock and they moved in and became co-owners of the farm in 1923.[8] Bessie, being a Whitlock, very familiar with the farm and having played a significant role as a young farm girl in the development of the farm, was now in a position to help care for Grace. Now Grace Whitlock had the following individuals to share her life and home: Clare, her husband; her three daughters (Viola, Alma and Medora); her younger brother Howard and his wife Bessie and their son Walter, born one year after Medora in 1923, and her mother Arvilla Whitney. The joining of the two families together initiated life-long relationships that succeeding generations still marvel at with respect to the caring, cooperation, and courtesy that existed in the big brick house on the corner: God's grace (Grace) in action.

> Ephesians 4:1, 2. I urge you to live a life worthy of the calling you have received. Be completely humble and gentle; be patient, bearing with one another in love. Make every effort to keep the unity of the Spirit through the bond of peace.

> "I am convinced as true religion or holiness cannot be without cheerfulness, so steady cheerfulness, on the other hand, cannot be without holiness and true religion. And I am equally convinced that true religion has nothing sour, austere, unsociable, unfriendly in it; but on the contrary, implies the most willing sweetness, the most amiable softness and gentleness."[9]

Grace had difficulties with her health, certainly related to pregnancy and birthing her girls. She had problems with high blood pressure and heart problems throughout her life. In 1934, Grace had a very serious illness related to a yellow skin tone that developed into the need for gall bladder surgery. Forty-seven days after her surgery on July 22, Grace went to church for the first time.[10]

Grace Whitlock, although small in stature and gentle in manner, had strong beliefs which she practiced in child care and development. She shared these with others by giving knowledgeable advice based on her experiences. These skills were essential in the care of her daughters and their families (Chapters 8-10).

> God has given us responsibility to choose what we invite into our hearts. We can choose to focus on God and take in messages of beauty, hope, joy, and courage. Or we can choose to take in messages of pessimism and cynicism. Whichever direction we lean will determine the type of heart we grow. Only a heart that trusts in God can praise him and reflect his glory to others.[11]

Grace chose to grow a heart of beauty, hope, joy, and courage. She loved the beauty of God's creation as exhibited in the Five Mile Valley and reflected in her passion for the creation of beautiful, crocheted doilies. The presence of these doilies on the furniture of friends and family certainly indicted the presence of Grace Whitlock.

.God gave Grace a heart of courage to continue the rest of her life assisting and comforting friends and relatives after her husband's death. Clare Whitlock died in 1943, just two months after his brother, Ray (Chapter 6). Unfortunately, Clare's will did not specifically provide a home for Grace since it was "understood" that Grace could remain in the big farm house co-owned by her brother Howard and Bessie Whitney (Clare's sister). Grace spent the rest of her life there with periodic trips to her daughters, usually lasting approximately six months in duration. Grace never remarried and was a widow for 27 years. During her life time, God provided hope and joy and the courage to be a comfort to relatives and friends since she outlived her husband; a brother-in-law and most of his son's family; a son-in-law, a daughter, and a grandchild.

At the age of 80, Grace still attended and was a member of her home church, the Five Mile Baptist Church. On Sunday evening, August 16, 1970, before the sermon, Pastor Harry Taylor gave the opportunity for anyone to recite their favorite Bible verse. Grace recited:

I Peter 2:24: He himself bore our sins in his body on the tree, so that we might die to sins and live for righteousness; by his wounds you have been healed.

Just minutes later during the sermon, Grace suddenly slumped over in the pew. Nancy Chesebro, her granddaughter, who was sitting next to her, immediately stretched Grace out in the pew and initiated CPR.[12] An ambulance was called, but Nancy knew that it was too late. Grace Potter Albright, who was named after her grandmother Grace Whitlock, perhaps said it best about the scripture that her grandmother recited. "How appropriate that those words would have been in her final thoughts. Christ's redemption, our only hope. That is the true source of the legacy that we have and all the great blessings that God's grace (and God's Grace-added by author) has showered upon us."What a way to spend the last minutes of one's life: giving testimony to God's grace of salvation!

Grace Olivia Whitney Whitlock was pronounced dead of a heart attack on arrival at St. Francis Hospital in Olean, New York. Grace was buried next to her husband in the Five Mile Cemetery.

Reasons for the inclusion of Grace Olivia Whitney Whitlock in this book about saints will be even more evident in the next three chapters in which she humbly showed God's grace and love to her three daughters during tragedies in their lives.

"Father, the message we get in our culture today is, Be strong! But you tell us that we're wise to admit our weakness, run to you, and wait to see your power and strength worked out in our frail beings. May our children see your strength because they see us turning to you in times of need. Amen."[13]

Top: (left to right) Viola Fern Whitlock Dunham, Grace Olivia
Whitney Whitlock; Middle: Alma Maud Whitlock Chesebro Rex
Bottom: Medora Orvilla Whitlock Potter 1943. Dunham Collection

8

Viola Fern Whitlock Dunham

Although the March 16, 1914, issue of the *Olean Times Herald* pictured spring fashions and a welcome weather report of moderating temperatures, a struggle for life was occurring in the brick house on the Five Mile Road in Allegany.[1] The struggle involved the mother Grace Whitlock and her baby daughter. The girl, who would be named Viola Fern Whitlock, was born at 8:15 PM and weighed 7 pounds "dressed" and was 21 inches long. "Viola had a hard struggle to live but is coming in fine shape. Had colic real bad until three months old. Eyes were blue until nearly a year old and then turned brown."[2] In addition to her parents, Clare and Grace Whitlock, Viola's grandparents, Stanley and Medora Linderman Whitlock, were still living in the house on the corner. When Viola was nine years old (1923), Howard and Bessie Whitlock Whitney moved into the house and became partners on the farm.[3]

Based on Viola's activities in her preteen and teen years, living in this multifamily situation shaped her life in many important areas: the importance of family, a strong work ethic, the acceptance of responsibilities, the importance of education, the development and care of friends, a strong belief and trust in God, and a mission for the effective spreading of Christ's gospel.

A major part of Viola's upbringing was centered in Christianity and the church. The fashion society of the 1920's had an emphasis on the "Sunshine Look." In addition to dress designs, the "look" also included etiquette and culture. During this time, a number of churches developed Sunshine classes for girls in which they were trained in etiquette and culture in a Christian context. Viola, age 14, was a member of such a class that held a supper meeting on Wednesday, March 16, 1926. The room was decorated for St. Patrick's Day and following the supper, the girls enjoyed games and music.[4]

Most of the church organizations for young people stressed the memorization of scripture, an activity also emphasized in the Whitlock home. During the 1920's, the Sunday School of the Five Mile Baptist Church sponsored a scripture verse program in which the students memorized verses and their context in the program. On July 14, 1928, it was announced in the *Olean Times Herald* that three girls were given top awards for their excellent memory of the required program: Viola Whitlock (age 14), Alma Whitlock (age 11, Viola's sister), and Lucille Dunham (age 17).[5] Scripture memorization remained important to Viola throughout her life as evidenced by her teaching in the home and church and by her involvement in AWANA, a Christian organization for young people based on Bible memorization.

The teaching of the importance of education by her parents culminated in Viola's graduation from Allegany High School on June 22, 1931.[6] An excellently worded, welcoming salutatory address to parents was given by Viola Fern Whitlock. Viola was very interested in teaching as a career and, following a summer of work around the farm, she was accepted into and joined the Teacher Training Class in Olean, New York. When the winter wind and snow made travel from the Five Mile to Olean impossible, Viola would stay overnight with her grandfather and grandmother, Stanley and Medora Whitlock, on Maple Street in Allegany. In her later years, she often recalled her fondness for her grandfather and Christian missions which grew from these visits.[7]

2 Timothy 3:14-17 But as for you, continue in what you have learned and have become convinced of, because you know those from whom you learned it, and how from infancy you have known the holy Scriptures, which are able to make you wise for salvation through faith in Christ Jesus. All Scripture is

God-breathed and is useful for teaching, rebuking, correcting and training in righteousness, so that the people of God may be thoroughly equipped for every good work.[8]

Through church attendance, Viola became acquainted with Verne Dunham, a neighbor on the Five Mile Road. Verne began to appear on the Whitlock farm to assist Viola in getting to school in Olean and to work on Viola's Model T Ford. They were married on May 7, 1932 in Rushford, New York.[8] At the time, Viola was teaching in a one-room school in Fitch, New York, and Verne had completed a two-year seminary program at Houghton College, Houghton, New York. After much prayer by the couple and relatives, they were called into God's ministry at the First Baptist Church, Cherry Creek, New York, on May 23, 1934.[9]

Joshua 24:14, 15 Now fear the Lord and serve him with all faithfulness, As for me and my household, we will serve the Lord.

"If God writes opportunity on one side of the door, he writes responsibility on the other."[10]

Romans 10: 14, 15 How, then, can they call on the one they have not believed in? And how can they believe in the one of whom they have not heard? And how can they hear without someone preaching to them? And how can they preach unless they are sent? As it is written, how beautiful are the feet of those who bring good news!

Viola became a dedicated pastor's wife who was supportive of the ministry in Cherry Creek, New York (1934-1943); Westfield, New York (1943-1946); Lorain, Ohio (1946-1959); Castile, New York (1959-1962); and a return to Lorain, Ohio (1962-1971). In all of these churches, she was active in women's missionary societies, Sunday school teaching, choir member, summer youth programs, area and statewide women's organizations, and ladies aid societies. During this period of time, she was blessed with four children: the first and only girl, Vaughn DeEtte Dunham (1937), after which Viola was seriously ill with uremic poisoning; a boy,

Valgene Loren Dunham (1940) and twin boys, Virgil Wesley Dunham and Verlee Clare Dunham (1944). All of her children became Christians, were baptized by their father, and all were educated beyond college with graduate degrees.[11]

I am sure that during these years, there were days when Viola may have felt tired and too busy in God's calling as a minister's wife and mother. Viola Whitlock Dunham had two aspects of the Holy Spirit's anointing, as described by Lloyd Ogilvie. The first aspect of anointing, salvation in Christ, signified by our baptism, sets us free to begin our Christian lives and growth in Christ. The second aspect of anointing is special "for each demanding opportunity."

> When we face complexities, we are given wisdom; when we are challenged to love unlovely people, we are given the gift of gracious love; when we are pressed to lead others into the unknown future, we are given vision and guidance. Each stretching possibility brings us back to the Lord for fresh anointing to break ground in the unexplored territory others are unwilling or afraid to pioneer.[12]

After 37 years in the ministry, retirement was considered with options included living on Morgan Hollow Road, where the Dunhams had a lake and cottages, or doing some type of "missionary" work at a slower pace. The couple communicated with the Fellowship of Baptists for Home Missions (FBHM), headquartered in Elyria, Ohio. FBHM provided pastors to congregations that met in homes or in rented space and did not have their own church building.

Verne and Viola accepted a position in Dover, Delaware, and moved into a mobile home provided for them. They arrived at their new pastorate on December 3, 1971, at 11:30 AM. On Sunday, December 5, attendance in a rented church was 20 in Sunday School and 18 in the morning and evening services.[13]

In the middle of January 1972, a site was located and approved, as well as permission to continue renting the current facility until the owner found a buyer or the church was ready to move. Planning and design followed with construction beginning in September.

On October 20th, Verne went to the church lot to assist in the planning of the heating systems. Viola, who knew that two of her children and their spouses were coming the next day to help build the church, spent the day cleaning, washing and cooking.

Saturday, October 21 dawned with a predicted temperature of 48 degrees and fit for major construction by men who had been planning for this day.

In Viola's words from her diary, October 21: " Men went to church lot at 7:10 AM. At 10:50 AM Verne fell-striking his head on cement floor. Unconscious till his death at Wilmington at 3:45 PM."[14] Robert John, a deacon, an eye witness, reported that during the construction of the rafters, Verne stepped forward on the auditorium floor to hand his son-in-law a spacer. In the process, Verne stepped too far and fell through the hole left for the baptistery, falling nine feet to the cement below. Verne was transferred first to Kent General Hospital in Dover by ambulance, which arrived only six minutes after the fall. Because of his failing condition, he was transferred in the afternoon to Wilmington, where he died. The next day, Sunday, Viola and family were in church for the morning worship. A woman of the church said that Viola was there Sunday morning to "comfort us." Viola had learned from her mother, Grace Whitlock that comfort comes in comforting. A memorial service was held (rental church) at 3 PM.[15]

> 2 Corinthians 1:3-4 Praise be to the God and Father of our Lord Jesus Christ, the Father of compassion and the God of all comfort, who comforts us in all our troubles, so that we can comfort those who are in any trouble with the comfort we ourselves have received from God.

Following the funeral service in Allegany at 2 PM on October 25, attendees went to the grave site at the Five Mile Cemetery. As people were leaving the cemetery, Viola did something that I will never forget. She called all of her children and their spouses together and said that all of us had been involved in sports during our lives and that she wanted us to form a football huddle. Not knowing what she was going to ask, I can remember forming the huddle with some confusion and uncertainty. She then wanted us to cheer because death did not have the victory, thanks to Christ's resurrection. I remember her counting to three and I yelled something, perhaps "Yeah," but I was still in a daze from the shock of my father being gone. My major regret about my father's untimely death is that I never had the opportunity to talk with him as an adult. I do remember thinking and still do, that this lady, Viola Whitlock Dunham, really lived what she believed.

> Isaiah 25:6-8. On this mountain the Lord Almighty will prepare a feast of rich food for all peoples, a banquet of aged wine—the best of meats and the finest of wines. On this mountain he will destroy the shroud that enfolds all peoples, the sheet that covers all nations; He will swallow up death forever. The Sovereign Lord will wipe away the tears from all faces.

Viola was now faced with life back in the Five Mile without a husband. Viola turned to the Lord and His service. Communication with the FBHM indicated the possibility of continued involvement in building new Baptist churches. An opportunity arose for her to be involved in a new church (22 members) in Wellsville, New York, about 30 miles from Allegany and about 45 minutes to one hour by car. She would be doing visitation, teaching the primary Sunday school class and other work related to young people. She accepted the position and went to Wellsville to begin her ministry there on January 10, 1973.[16]

On August 3, 1974, Viola made a serious decision to be involved with FBHM at their office in Elyria, Ohio. She went to Lorain to learn aspects of office work and lived with Jeanette Langthorp, a longstanding friend of the family. During 1975-1980, no diaries are available, but Viola saw several changes in her life. She was quite busy in Ohio while working for FBHM and visited many churches in support of FBHM. In addition, Viola served numerous women's groups by giving talks on how to build a happy home and patterns for Christian living. She retired from active office work for FBHM in Ohio and returned to her cottage at the lake in New York.

Nineteen eighty-one began the rest of Viola's life. She now was officially retired and was now ready to serve God through her ministry of letter writing, visits to the needy and ill, and visits to her children and their families. She continued activity in the her home church and also began an active child care program in which she had scheduled days spent at the children's homes.[17]

Because of a severely broken ankle in a fall and other difficulties she faced living alone, she sold all of her property and moved to 3469 Five Mile Road, about one mile from the big red brick house where she was born. Viola's schedule books indicate that she was active in church related opportunities, such as AWANA, choir, and in the Christmas programs for 1989.

When she was 80 years old (1994), she put aside her Sunday School teaching of young girls. Several mishaps at her home indicated that she needed special care, and she was happy to move to Eden Heights Assisted Living in Olean, New York (1997), where a few of her friends were living.[18]

In Eden Heights she was free to go visiting with relatives and friends who provided the transportation. On several of these occasions, she told stories about her life in Eden Heights that indicated that she was imagining things which were not happening but were very real to her. An analysis of the letters that Viola wrote to Frank and Vaughn Dunham Estep during her stay in Eden Heights indicates that Viola's dementia was increasing. This person who had the ability to put correctly-spelled words together in a very coherent manner was now having trouble spelling, was very repetitious in her letters, and child-like in telling the stories of her existence at Eden Heights.[19]

As her symptoms of dementia increased, she was put under doctor's care and was transferred to Pines Healthcare and Rehabilitation Center in Olean. I remember very vividly that last time I saw my mother. She looked at me with horror on her face and I perceived some tears in her eyes. She said nothing at all when my name was mentioned. I don't know if she didn't know me and thought that she should, or she knew me and wanted to speak but could not.

Viola died at the Pines Healthcare and Rehabilitation Center in Olean, New York, on November 24, 2005, age 91. At her death she had been blessed with four children, seven grandchildren and seven great grandchildren. Visitors were welcomed at the Five Mile Baptist Church from noon to 2 PM on Tuesday, November 29, with the service starting at 2 PM. Not many people have their funeral service in their home church just across the street from the house in which they were born.

At the funeral I spoke about wondering how God spoke peace to Viola through the clouds of Alzheimer's. I said I didn't know but now Viola could speak face to face with her Lord. It almost seems the author of the hymn "Face to Face with Christ my Savior" had my mother's Alzheimer's in mind when she wrote:

> "What rejoicing in His presence when are banished grief and pain;
> When the crooked ways are straightened and the dark things shall be plain.
> Face to face I shall behold Him, far beyond the starry sky;
> Face to face in all His glory, I shall see Him by and by!"[20]

One of God's multi-talented servants, Viola Fern Whitlock Dunham, left relatives and hundreds of friends with the knowledge that they had witnessed an example of Christ's two commandments from the New Testament,

> Matthew 22:37-40. "Love the Lord your God with all your heart and with all your soul and with all your mind. This is the first and greatest commandment. And the second is like it: Love your neighbor as yourself. All the Law and the Prophets hang on these two commandments."

Viola Fern Whitlock Dunham had faithfully served God and His people in six different churches from 1934 to 1972. Supported by God and her family and friends, she was able to survive the tragic loss of her husband and live for God for another 33 years until her passing.

> "The golden evening brightens in the west;
> Soon, soon to faithful warriors cometh rest;
> And sweet the calm of Paradise, the blest.
> Alleluia! Alleluia![21]

9

Alma Maud Whitlock Chesebro Rex

A discussion of the life of Alma Whitlock might initially focus on her size. "Sometimes, ...the smallest things take up the most room in your heart;"[1] "God blessed me with a lot of heart and no height, and I'd take that any day;"[2] "God only lets things grow until they're perfect. Some of us didn't take as long as others;" the old adage "Good things come in small packages."

Alma started out small. Since her mother, Grace Whitlock, had a difficult delivery of her first daughter, Viola, her parents may have planned that the delivery of their second child would be in a hospital. Alma Maud Whitlock started to arrive one month early, so Grace was taken to Higgins Memorial Hospital in Olean, New York. Alma arrived at 1:20 PM on Friday, February 9, 1917, weighing four pounds and four ounces and was 19 inches in height. As expected for a premature baby in 1917, mother and child had a difficult time and were in the hospital for three weeks and three days.

When Grace and Alma left the hospital, Alma weighed four pounds and thirteen ounces. Just like Viola, Alma had a serious case of colic, but when treated with medication prescribed by Dr. Gould, along with some of Grandma's catnip tea, she became "fat and pretty with real blue eyes and red hair."[3] Because of her size, she was kept in an open dresser drawer and not in a cradle.[4] Her first smiles and vocal "Goos" occurred when she was nine weeks old, weighing approximately seven pounds. She recognized her hands at the age of three months when she weighed eight pounds and 14 ounces. She could hold her head up at four months of age and weighed ten pounds. When the Whitlocks celebrated Alma's first birthday, she weighed 16 pounds.[5]

The Whitlocks introduced Alma to the relatives and the community just as soon as the mother and child felt ready to attend church. Early family gatherings focused on readings from scripture and devotions. On August 15, 1919, at age two, Alma attended the Trowbridge/Whitlock Reunion in Ischua with her parents and older sister.[6]

> "Jesus, Son of human mother, Bless our motherhood, we pray; Give us grace to lead our children, Draw them to Thee day by day; May our sons and daughters be Dedicated, Lord, to Thee."[7]

> "Happy the home where Jesus' name is sweet to every ear; Where children early lisp His fame, and parents hold Him dear."[8]

Close ties were made between Viola and Alma, just three years apart. These ties continued throughout their lives. Although they were sometimes separated by space, they never broke these ties which were characterized by love and support. In her later years as a widow, Alma visited her older sister almost daily. The two sisters could be seen together at family reunions, church, shops, women's meetings, and trips to see relatives. When friends and relatives came to visit, both sisters entertained. For certain, the two sisters could be seen at their favorite restaurants in Olean, Portville and Allegany after church on Sundays.[9]

As an infant and growing child, Alma Whitlock was presented with love, not only from her family, but also from God through her exposure to the Bible at home and at the Five Mile Baptist Church. In the Whitlock household, Alma was exposed to music, often centered on classical music or hymns of the church. She and her older sister learned to play the piano and often sang together, including at church and at funerals.[10] Alma grew up in the church on the Five Mile and remained an active member her entire life. She could be counted on to be involved in Sunday School, first as a student and then as a teacher. For many years she served God and her fellow members by playing the piano and organ in worship services.

> "For the joy of ear and eye, For the heart and mind's delight,
> For the mystic harmony Linking sense to sound and sight,
> Lord of all, to Thee we raise This our hymn of grateful praise."[11]

In the Whitlock household, the scriptures were an important part of daily life. Just like her older sister Viola, Alma was expected to learn the stories of the Bible and to memorize important verses. She was quite skilled at memorization as indicted by her being awarded one of the top prizes in a Sunday School memorization program when she was 11 years old. She competed with Viola, age 14 and Lucille Dunham, age 17.[12]

When Alma was five years old she gained another set of "parents" when Howard and Bessie Whitney moved in to the house on the corner. At this time, the Whitneys had no children of their own. So at an early age, Alma was exposed to the wonderful world of books and the Scriptures by her mother Grace as well as "Aunt" Bessie. Both of these women and their husbands, even though busy with the farm, were supportive of education in the home as well as serving on local school boards. Alma did well in school and graduated from Allegany High School on June 26, 1934, at the age of 17.[13]

By this time Alma was exposed to a number of choices for her future that were created by her situation. Her performance in school, having an older sister who was a school teacher, and interested parents, may have combined to provide an interest toward education. She certainly had "assigned" duties as well as being an older sister and friend to younger sister, Medora. There is no doubt that Alma knew her way around the farm because she was often called to assist in farm chores, including milking, when other members of the family were ill.[14]

For a farm girl of 17, with an older sister teaching school and responsibilities on the farm and in the house, any social activity was almost entirely related to the church. One year before Alma's graduation, Bert Chesebro, age 61, became a Christian and he and his family joined the Five Mile Baptist Church. Bert and Lena Chesebro were the parents of seven children. Their fifth child, Kenneth Bert Chesebro, was born on November 15, 1915.[15] Kenneth attended the Humphrey District Number 3 one-room schoolhouse on the corner of Church and Five Mile Roads. In the 1930's western New York, as well as other parts of the world, suffered through an epidemic of polio. Ken survived a period of time in an iron lung in Olean, New York, and a stressful time in therapy, to become a strong, healthy young man. Alma must have heard early on about Ken, who was mentioned in prayer requests at church. Ken had recovered and was dating Alma at the big house on the corner by 1932.

Alma Whitlock was married to Kenneth Chesebro three years later on February 22, 1935, at 7:45 PM in the parsonage of the Five Mile Baptist Church on Church Road. The honeymoon certainly was not extravagant and expensive because the couple had little in the way of finances. They spent their honeymoon at her sister in Cherry Creek, New York, and then to Ken's sisters. Ken and Alma returned home for a short visit on the night of Monday, March 4. The next day, Kenneth was at work in the sugar bush and tapped about 350 buckets of sap.[16]

March 6, 1935 was a very important day for Alma Whitlock Chesebro. That afternoon the big house on the corner was full of visitors for a reception for Alma. Friday, March 8, dawned with clear skies but only 10 degrees above zero and snow covering the ground. Ken and Alma met with Clare Whitlock to determine their future. Clare already knew that his new son-in-law was trustworthy and hard working. He hired Ken and Alma by the month and most importantly was told by Ken that in the future, when able, the newly-weds would eventually like to have Frank Whitlock's farm in Morgan Hollow. These decisions proved to be a commitment for both Alma and Ken to assist on the Whitlock/Whitney farm and provided a residence for the couple. For a brief time they resided in the big house on the corner but moved to the tenant house just up the Morgan Hollow Road.[17]

Alma and Ken became very active in the Five Mile Baptist Church, which included regular attendance, music, and Sunday School teaching. For example, on November 6, 1935, they hosted the church's prayer meeting at their house.[18]

The year 1936 did not start off too well for Alma Chesebro. On

January 20, Bessie took Alma to the doctor in Olean. It was determined that she needed an immediate operation which was performed on January 22. The removal of her gall bladder started at 9:00 AM and took 40 minutes. After receiving care from her mother, Grace Whitlock, she moved back to her home.[19]

Alma recovered and was able to host a party for her Sunday School class on March 12. Finally, after having chills and a fever on March 21, Alma was well enough to attend church the next day with the family.[20]

On the night of December 19, 1936, Ken took Alma and her mother, Grace, to Olean, and Alma checked into the hospital and gave birth to a daughter at 5:00 AM on December 20. Esther Mae Chesebro weighed seven pounds and ten ounces and Alma was as well "as could be expected." Grace went to the Chesebro's house to greet them and stayed there to assist the new mother. The new father was out cutting poles and plowing Frank Whitlock's fields.[21]

Alma was quite busy taking care of Esther in January, 1937. She was assisted by her mother, Grace, and younger sister Medora. On January 4, 1937, a cold Sunday morning, Ken and Alma took Esther to church for the first time.

During the next two years, Alma was busy raising Esther, teaching Sunday School, and filling in when needed at the big farm.

On May 12, 1939, Harlan Leroy Chesebro was born. "Mike," as he was called the rest of his life, was a hard-working individual even as a pre-teenager. After the death of her father, Clare Whitlock, in 1943, Alma inherited property on Karl Road. While working on the big farm, Ken and Alma were able to gain some independence by moving from the tenant house to a small cabin on Karl Road. The Chesebros then began to plan and initiate the construction of the Chesebro farm in which their children grew up. The house was built by hand by Ken, friends, and relatives that could assist.

Alma was raising two children, helping on the big farm on the corner and also in the building of her home of the future. With the establishment of a productive dairy farm, the Chesebros now spent less time working on the Whitlock/Whitney farm.

The family grew with the birth of another boy, Donavan Clare

Chesebro, on July 8, 1946. As expected, Alma's mother Grace, who was now a widow, was there to assist with the new baby. Alma had a fourth child, Stephen Bert Chesebro, three years later in 1949.

In the early 1950's, Esther was doing very well at Allegany High School and wished to go on to college and become a teacher like her Aunts Viola and Medora had been. Realizing the family's financial situation, Alma began to work outside the home in housekeeping to earn extra funds for Esther's education.[22] This work Alma accomplished as mother of four children, her service to her church and community, and her help with Ken on a successful dairy farm. Because of Alma's support, Esther was able to attend the new Christian college in Ohio, Cedarville College. After a career as a pastor's wife and high school teacher in Indiana, she retired from the public schools and continued as Adjunct Professor in Education at Indiana-Purdue University in Indianapolis (Indianapolis University).[23]

Tuesday, September 19, 1961, started for Don (age 15) and Steve (age 12) like a normal school day. After returning from school, they started doing their chores. During milking time, their father rushed into the barn and told them that their bull had broken through the fence and was pursuing a heifer on someone else's property. The three of them jumped on the big Ford tractor with Ken driving. As darkness began to settle, the tractor, traveling on rough terrain, hit a large rock and overturned. The boys were fortunate to be thrown clear of the tractor, but it came down and crushed the chest of their father. Alma, who was attending a Sunday School meeting at church, was called. Ambulances had been called, but it was too late. Alma, age 44, had lost her strong, supportive husband who had overcome polio and had lead his family in bringing their children up in a Christian atmosphere and doing the right thing in the community. The extended Whitlock and Whitney families were there to assist Alma and her children.[24]

> "When peace like a river attendeth my way,
> When sorrows like sea billows roll:
> Whatever my lot, Thou has taught me to say,
> It is well, it is well with my soul."[25]

After the funeral, Alma must have had many occasions in which she looked at her situation in life. Her mother Grace had now been a widow for 18 years, and Alma may have wondered about her own opportunities for remarriage. Alma realized that farming was impossible under these circumstances and took advantage of a lease option to lease the livestock and farm and retain the house as residence for her family.[26]

> Jeremiah 29:11 For I know the plans I have for you, declares the Lord, plans for welfare and not for evil, to give you a future and a hope.

When Don and Steve needed a haircut, Alma had taken the boys to a barbershop on Main Street in Allegany. The barber was a short, pleasant Christian man named Milo Rex (age 59), who had lost his first wife, Gertrude (age 65), in 1961. A friendship developed between Milo and Alma that resulted in love and marriage in April of 1962. Some may have wondered if the marriage was too soon after Ken's death, but in the minds of Alma's nieces and nephews who got to know Milo, he appeared to be the perfect husband for Alma.[27]

Alma continued to minister through her Sunday School class and her musical talents at the Five Mile Baptist Church. Her marriage to Milo provided her comfort during another stressful time in her life when Stephen, her youngest son, was drafted into the Army and sent to Vietnam in the late spring of 1970.[28]

Viola recorded on January 1, 1981, that Milo had been ill but was some better. Unfortunately, just two days later, Milo was barely alive and only semiconscious. During this time Viola was very supportive, and Alma's daughter-in-law, Nancy, took her to see Milo in the hospital. Through a period of very cold weather in the first two weeks of 1981, Milo fought for life. On January 18, 1981, Alma lost her second husband, Milo Rex at about noon. January 21, 1981, was a beautiful sunny day with everything covered with frost. Milo's funeral was at the Five Mile Baptist Church at 1:30 PM.[29]

"And Lord, haste the day when the faith shall be sight,
The clouds be rolled back as a scroll,
The trump shall resound and the Lord shall descend,
Even so—it is well with my soul."[30]

Later that evening, the two sisters went to prayer meeting. This family had learned that the best way to be comforted was to show their love and comfort to others. Consequently, Viola and Alma went to Salamanca just two days after the funeral to see Lucille Nudd, Viola's sister-in-law, who was in a care facility.

The excellent times Alma had with her family were very supportive for a woman who had lost two husbands and perhaps prepared her for additional tragedy. On a lovely Sunday, June 7, 1992, after church services that involved communion, Alma was informed that her eldest son, Mike, had suffered a heart attack. After a short stay at home, Mike was back in the hospital, and five days later was in intensive care with an infected spleen. On July 13, he was taken to Rochester and had CAT scans taken the next day.

On July 23, Alma was home and Mike seemed to be progressing after surgery to repair a hole in his stomach lining and to clean infected areas. On Thursday, August 27, 1992, a very weak and feeble Harlan Leroy "Mike" Chesebro came home to be with Janice and their family. Mike died three weeks later on Thursday, September 17th. Monday, September 21st, was a rainy day for the funeral at the Five Mile Baptist Church. The service started at 1:00 PM with scripture reading and prayer, followed by the grave committal at the church. Over one hundred guests were served lunch.[31]

His grandson, Michael Edward "Mike" Chesebro, while a fifth grader, wrote a beautiful note entitled "A Gift of Heart" in which he offered his heart to his grandfather.

A Gift of Heart

The best gift I would give away is my heart. I would give to my grandfather because he died of a heart attack. It would be wrapped in red paper with a shiny red bow. My grandfather would open it and have a new heart. He would feel good because he has a new heart. I would feel great because I gave him back his life.[32]

The new year, 1993, started as it should; the two sisters had supper together at Alma's on Friday, January 1. With no warning, Don, Alma's second oldest son, appears in Viola's diary on July 20. That day Viola took Alma to see Don who was in the hospital. The next day the sisters started the prayer chain at church for Don who was in the hospital at Roswell in Buffalo with a growth in the pancreas. That evening when Alma returned from the hospital, the two sisters went to the cemetery to water flowers on a "cool and lovely evening." Donavan Clare Chesebro died in the early morning of July 30, 1993, at the young age of 47.[33] Alma came to Viola's for lunch. Don's funeral at the Five Mile Baptist Church was held on August 2, followed by dinner and visiting. The next day Esther and the two sisters visited Dorothy Chesebro in Rew, Pennsylvania. Comfort from comforting!

Alma Maud Chesebro Rex had now lost two husbands, one by accident, two sons long before their expected lifespan, and a third son who had survived heavy fighting in Vietnam. Through all of these trials and problems, Alma remained pleasant, joyful, and supportive of friends and relatives who needed and sought her affection. Except for when they were traveling separately, the two Whitlock sisters leaned on each other and saw each other or talked by phone most every day. Those of us who were fortunate to know the sisters well, can just image the conversations the sisters had as they went for rides in the countryside and passed numerous farms of people they had known earlier in their lives.

The remainder of Viola's last diary (1995) indicates that the two sisters continued to communicate almost every day. Letters of Viola's to Frank and Vaughn Estep after she moved to Eden Heights in Olean, New York, indicated that Viola was losing her mental abilities. Alma, age 80, visited Viola as often as possible. She was still driving her own car and kept Viola up to date concerning church activities and family matters, even though the news may not have registered in her sister's mind. What did register in Viola's mind is that she thought Alma was too old to be driving. The sisters talked by telephone almost every day, and most of Viola's letters indicated just how important Alma was to her daily happiness and security.[34]

As the days passed for Alma, she too had trouble remembering things. When the time was right, determined primarily by her daughter-in-law Nancy, attempts were made to have Alma live with Viola at Eden Heights in Olean, New York. However, no space was available at that time.

After a month of effort, red tape, and no available rooms at Pines Health Care-Olean with Viola, Nancy was able to find a room for Alma in Pines Healthcare-Machias. Alma brought her Christian testimony even as her mind continued to fail. She was called the "church lady" because she was always witnessing to her neighbors. Not only did she attend the Baptist services, but she went with a Catholic friend to mass.[35]

The last time I saw my Aunt Alma was at my mother's (Viola) memorial service at the Five Mile Baptist Church, just after Thanksgiving in 2005. There was an important picture taken that day. Alma, and her son, Stephen Chesebro, who would be her only surviving child, were photographed with the author and his siblings.

On February 23, 2008, Esther Mae Chesebro Smith, Alma's first child and Clare and Grace Whitlock's first grandchild, died in Indiana. Her funeral was held at the Gasburg Baptist Church on March 1, 2008, where Esther had been an active member for many years. Esther was buried next to her husband Billy at the West Newton Cemetery.[36]

Alma Maud Whitlock Chesebro Rex died on the day before Christmas, 2008, at Pines Healthcare-Machias. She had experienced tragedy and great blessings in her life and outlived two husbands, three of her four children, and one grandchild. Surviving were Stephen Chesebro, her youngest child, 11 grandchildren and 17 great grandchildren. She is buried next to Kenneth in the Five Mile Cemetery, the fences of which she had painted.[37] In a poem by Frank Topping entitled "Bedtime," the author asks God for peace and rest after recognizing that it was God who had directed to the current "time and place."[38]

"God His own doth tend and nourish; In His holy courts they flourish.

From all evil things He spares them; In His mighty arms He bears them.

Though He giveth or He taketh, God His children ne'er forsaketh; His the loving purpose solely To preserve them pure and holy."[39]

10

Medora Orvilla Whitlock Potter

Jeremiah 29:11 For I know the plans I have for you, declares the Lord, plans to prosper you and not to harm you, plans to give you hope and a future.

The *Olean Evening Herald*, Olean, New York, printed weather headlines of unsettled conditions with showers in the evening for August 23, 1922.[1] The weather was not the only unsettled event that day. Prayers were being asked and answered for unsettled conditions at the hospital; prayers were for Grace Whitlock as she gave birth to her third child. Just like her older sister Alma, Medora arrived early and weighed only three pounds and thirteen ounces. For awhile the expectation was that neither Grace nor Medora would survive. Much later when Medora's oldest son David was discussing his mother's birth, his family physician asked if Medora's parents were Christians. After an affirmative answer, David remembers his doctor saying that in 1922, love played a significant force in survival of a premature infant.[2] Medora didn't walk until she was 17 months of age, but did say several words earlier when she was one year old.[3]

The big brick farmhouse was now the residence of two families, the Whitlocks and the Whitneys. Medora came home from the hospital to join her parents and two older sisters, Viola (age 8) and Alma (age 5). In addition, Howard and Bessie (Whitlock) Whitney moved into the house in 1923 and would have a baby boy, Walter Whitney, that same year.

Walter and Medora grew up in the same house, like a brother and sister, and were life-long friends.[4]

As with her two older sisters, Clare and Grace Whitlock introduced Medora to the family as soon as possible. This was accomplished in a Whitney family get-together in the fall of 1922 under the big elm trees. On August 14, 1925, Clare and Grace took their three girls to the Whitlock/Trowbridge reunion in Ischua, New York. At the age of five, Medora had the experience of a full Whitney reunion in 1927. It is expected that her two older sisters were helpful in getting to know the many relatives and friends of the two families. The two older sisters also set the example for learning household chores and the more than occasional work in the barns and henhouse. Part of Medora's early interests certainly came from the families' activities, not just in work, but in reading and in music. It is quite clear from Medora's diary of 1943, that she knew her relatives of both families and had developed a habit of letter writing characterized by love and caring. This apparently was true when she herself was under stress. Once again, comforting others resulted in comfort for each of the Whitlock sisters and their mother, Grace.

As soon as possible, Medora joined her family in Sunday school and church attendance at the Five Mile Baptist Church. On frequent occasions, church attendance helped her to learn and appreciate her many relatives that worshiped at the Five Mile Baptist Church.

> "Grant us then pure hearts and patient, That in all we do or say
> Little ones our deeds may copy, and be never led astray;
> Little feet our steps may follow In a safe and narrow way." [5]

In regular attendance at church, she must have observed that her family not only faithfully loved and studied the scriptures at home but also on Sundays and on prayer meeting nights. In the Whitlock/Whitney families, scripture reading and memorization were important, and Medora began a life-long memorization and love of the Bible. Later in life, her husband, Rev. Wesley Potter, called her his "walking Bible encyclopedia."[6] As a child she accepted Christ as her personal Savior and was baptized the same day as housemate, Walter Whitney, who had made the same decision.

At the age of 10, Medora's name began to appear in her father's earliest surviving diary (1932). Along with her sisters, she attended a Bible conference at Maplehurst, New York, on February 21 and 22. On a "fine, clear, warm day," June 28, the sisters attended a Sunday school picnic at Cuba Lake. She also accompanied her family when they went to Lime Lake for worship services that summer as well (July 24, 27-31, August 2, 5-7).

By the age of 12, Medora had proven that she was a very intelligent, quick learner and had extended her reading to almost anything in reach. As evidenced by her diary, she read assigned readings in school, newspapers (modeled after her entire family), as well as the scriptures. Although her older sisters (Viola, age 20; Alma, age 17), were a constant source of education and experience around the farm, she was now learning more on her own since her older sisters were finding interests outside the family.[7] As teenagers, Medora and Walt were involved in the chores around the farm, including special season-related tasks, such as corn husking, feed grinding (May 4, 1935), and wood gathering (January 27, 1935).

On January 31, perhaps due to exposure to cold weather, Medora became ill with the "grip." She was in bed with a fever of 104 degrees and a pulse rate of 120. The doctor was called to the house and treated her, along with her father and Bessie Whitney, for the same problems. Finally, after bouts with high temperatures while the outside temperatures were below zero, Medora was able play some board games (February). A close association with her mother served Medora well in the closeness that developed as her older sisters left the farm. Later in Medora's life, her mother Grace was very important in helping her around the house and loving and caring for her children.[8]

Medora and Walt were involved in weekly young people's meetings that were held at the church. This was in addition to the weekly prayer meeting on Wednesday nights. Both Medora and Walt were active in the music program of the church with piano playing by Medora and both of them involved vocally in solos and in groups.

In January of 1937, Grace and Medora were staying with Alma and her new baby Esther almost every evening. As a sophomore in high school, Medora was maintaining an excellent record while tending to sick relatives, working on the farm, being involved in numerous church activities, and supporting the Allegany Central School's basketball team. As usual, summer involved work on the farm, music at church, and family reunions.

> "When our growing sons and daughters Look on life with eager eyes, Grant us then a deeper insight And new pow'rs of sacrifice; Hope to trust them, faith to guide them, Love that nothing good denies." [9]

Medora's senior year at Allegany Central School culminated with Class night, June 24, 1940 and commencement the following evening. Class Night was an evening filled with music and special presentations. One of the presentations was a poem read by Medora Whitlock. A longer presentation was entitled "Side Glances of 1955." Each member of the class entered a rustic cottage on the stage to meet the President of the United States in 1955 and was introduced by what the other members of the class had thought that each student would be doing in 1955, fifteen years after their graduation. Her classmates estimated that Medora would be Superintendent at Buffalo General Hospital. This is one indication that Medora was thinking about a career in health care, specifically in nursing. [10]

The next evening the Commencement exercise for the class of 35 members took place at 8 PM. Medora Arvilla Whitlock gave the Valedictory speech. In the speech Medora reminded the audience of the citizens' responsibilities, especially as war clouds were covering the sky in Europe. When the United State entered the war, some of Medora's relatives, including her classmate and cousin, Stanley, risked their lives to "preserve the flame of civilization," not only here but in Europe as well.

The custom of that time was for graduating seniors to pass out name cards to those classmates that they wished to have comments written on the back. Eight of Medora's cards have survived with comments written on the back. A card was returned by one of her teachers and class advisor, Miss Irene J. Schnell. She wrote, "Dear Medora, For four years I have had you in class and never for a single moment have you been anything but a joy to me. That is a record. I shall miss the pert, attentive look which you always have. Good luck to the salutatorian." (signed) IJS (Medora's class standing was recalculated to valedictorian).[11]

The interest in nursing seems to have been decreased as her work around the farm increased. Medora had accepted household responsibilities, and almost every day she was involved in cleaning, washing, and keeping the fires. In addition, Grace, Bessie, and Medora had the extra responsibility for Clare, whose health was rapidly failing, and for Medora's grandmother, Arvilla Whitney. Medora had the responsibility of giving Clare an injection and was involved in changing bed linen for both father and grandmother. In addition, she was now keeping track of the farm's finances (including income taxes) because Clare was ill. When the men of the farm were doing seasonal work or butchering, Medora often joined Alma and assisted with the milking.[12]

About this time in 1943, the name of Wesley Raymond Potter began to appear in Medora's diary. Wesley graduated from Great Valley High School, Great Valley, New York, in 1940 and enrolled at Houghton College in preparation for the ministry.

As the involvement of the United States appeared to be increasing in the war in Europe, Wes wanted to support the United States and wished to enter officer's training school. While waiting for his orders that summer, he worked in an oil field. He was seriously injured in an accident and while in the hospital, his army orders came. Because his left arm had been permanently paralyzed, he could not be in the military and returned to Houghton College.[13]

At that time, the pulpit at the Five Mile Baptist Church was empty as the congregation searched for a new pastor. Because of the proximity of the college to the Five Mile, Wes was able to fill the pulpit as an intern on Sundays. If Wes was preaching on Sunday or leading the Young Peoples meetings, Medora took special interest and made comments in her diary.

Stress over her father's health also began to show in Medora's diary. On Monday, June 28, 1943, Medora wrote: "I stayed at the hospital all day. I was so tired—in fact I am so tired and disgusted with everyone at the hospital. I should have typed (family finances) but didn't feel up to it. Ken stayed with Pop (Clare Whitlock) tonight. Viola came to get me.

I hope I don't have to go to the hospital tomorrow." She did, out of love and respect for Pop.

Medora did not make any entries in the diary in the first week of July. On Wednesday July 7, she wrote "Pop died today at 10:40 A.M. in the St. Francis hospital." There were no entries on July 8 and 9. On Saturday, June 10, she wrote "Pop's funeral was today at 2:30 P.M." She wrote nothing else in 1943. No other diaries of Medora's have survived.

With Wes involved at Houghton College, Medora was thinking and praying about her future and employment. Upon graduating from Houghton in 1944, Wes was accepted for divinity studies at Northern Baptist Theological Seminary in Chicago, Illinois, in preparation for the ministry.[15] It appeared that Medora felt that her ministry might combine teaching with her faith in some manner, so she enrolled in a two-year program at Practical Bible Training School in Binghamton, New York in the fall of 1944 (currently Davis College). The school functioned in preparing individuals for ministry as music/worship leaders, teachers in various youth ministries with possible concentrations in Bible and theology. After two years of grades never less than 90 percent, this excellent student was now prepared for some type of Christian service in which her Biblical knowledge and understanding would be combined with her interest in people and teaching.[16]

> II Timothy 2:15 Do your best to present yourself to God as one approved, a workman who does not need to be ashamed and who correctly handles the word of truth.

In the 1940's, a group of business people in Cortland County, New York, supported the presence of Bible clubs in their schools and hired Medora Whitlock in the fall of 1946 to be a Bible Club Missionary and teach Religious Education. Medora taught under the Bible Club movement of Philadelphia, Pennsylvania, and worked in and around Cortland, New York.[17]

> Proverbs 4:13 Hold on to instruction, do not let it go; Guard it well, for it is your life.

Correspondence and visits continued between Medora and Wes and they decided to be married. Grace Whitlock sent out wedding invitations for Medora and Wes Potter and the wedding occurred on June 30, 1948, at the Five Mile Baptist Church. Her sisters, Viola and Alma, were bride maids. Howard Whitney gave the bride away in the absence of Medora's father. The reception was held at the big house on the corner for approximately 150 guests. The house was decorated with garden flowers and a miniature bride in the bay window. The newly-weds spent their honeymoon at Niagara Falls and the Thousand Islands and began their life together in an apartment at 525 Franklin Street, Danville, Illinois. They began their ministry together as assistant pastor and wife at the First Baptist Church in Danville.[18]

Wes and Medora became very busy in God's work. One of the projects that the new assistant pastor was assigned was to develop a mission church. Through hard work involving visitations, youth ministry, preaching, Sunday school teaching by both Medora and Wes, the Fowler Avenue Baptist Church (currently Edgewood Baptist) was established to the north of the parent church.[19]

In addition to the process of building a church family on Fowler Avenue, Wes and Medora began a family more close to home. On April 9, 1949, David Robert Potter was born. Medora became an excellent mother, especially in the area of reading and teaching the scriptures. David does not remember memorizing Psalm 23; "It seems that I have always known it by heart." On one occasion, when his father was out of town, Medora and David prayed together and David committed his heart to the Lord.[20]

Vernon Clare Potter arrived on October 10, 1951, to join two-year-old David, extending Medora's love for family and increasing her work load. The boys became the best of friends, excellent playmates and made acquaintances with other children in the neighborhood. The boys learned to obey their parents and to love God at this early age. One of the daily things that they learned around the house was that at a certain time each day they were to play quietly. That time was when their mother had her personal devotions during which she would read the Bible and pray.[21]

Proverbs 14:26. He who fears the Lord has a secure fortress, and for his children it will be a refuge.

Isaiah 38:3. Remember, O Lord, how I have walked before you faithfully and with wholehearted devotion and have done what is good in your eyes.

Medora's workload increased with the arrival of Grace Leora Potter on July 24, 1953. The Potters were very busy and happy with their three children and things were going well with the Fowler Avenue Baptist Church. In fact, it was now time to build a new church because of the increasing size of the congregation. Wes closely followed and was involved in the project, as much as his pastoral duties would allow. Some of the church members would assist in construction and would work in the late afternoon. Consequently, Wes often went to the site and unlocked the storage unit so that the workers would have access to tools and supplies.[22]

Tuesday, April 13, 1954, was expected to be slightly warm for Danville, 57 degrees, so that the Potter boys could play in the afternoon with the neighborhood children in the front yard. Wes had left the house to go unlock the storage unit for construction workers, and Medora was busy hanging up clothes to dry in the backyard.

A determination of what exactly happened is difficult, simply because the only family eye witness was David, age five. In combining the impressions of David, and what was passed on as family history, the following sad story has resulted.

Apparently the boys and neighborhood children were playing in their front yard at 1210 Jackson Street, a residential street with not too much traffic. A neighbor boy, about three or four years, apparently dared Vernon to run across the street and back. Vernon followed. Both of the boys went safely to the other side. On the way back, the neighbor ran across the street safely. Apparently, Vernon waited for a car to pass and ran into the street. He did not see a second car that was being driven by a teenager who was late for an appointment, taking a shortcut, and was speeding on this residential street.[23]

Vernon was rushed to the hospital. Wes was called, but before he could arrive at the hospital, Vernon was dead. David remembers that he and his father "cried rivers. Mom was completely dry-eyed. She needed the release of expressed sorrow and never got it."[24]

> Psalms 23:4, 6. Even though I walk through the valley of the shadow of death, I will fear no evil, for you are with me; thy rod and your staff, they comfort me. Surely goodness and love will follow me all the days of my life, and I will dwell in the house of the Lord forever.

> "Does Jesus care when my heart is pained too deeply for mirth and song;
> As the burdens press and the cares distress, And the way grows weary and long?
> O yes, He cares; I know He cares, His heart is touched with my grief;
> When the days are weary, the long nights dreary,
> I know my Savior cares."[25]

On April 16, 1954, Vernon's body arrived in Olean and was taken to the Potter family home in Humphrey. Funeral services were held on Saturday, April 17, 1954, in the Five Mile Baptist Church, officiated by pastor Rev. Victor Stouffer, and Rev. Dean Houser, pastor of the Humphrey Baptist Church. Vernon Clare Potter was buried in the Allegany Cemetery, Allegany, New York.[26]

Medora, who was three months pregnant at the time, suffered with the loss, and Wes, at one point, thought that she was having a nervous breakdown. Wes used the Christian principle that the Whitlock girls employed when tragedy struck. When you comfort others, you receive comfort. The scripture that Wes claimed at this time was II Corinthians 4:17, 18, a section written by the Apostle Paul concerning suffering within God's ministry. The author has added verse 16 as well.

II Corinthians 4:16-18 Therefore, we do not lose heart. Though outwardly we are wasting away, yet inwardly we are being renewed day by day. For our light and momentary troubles are achieving for us an eternal glory that far outweighs them all. So we fix our eyes not on what is seen, but on what is unseen. For what is seen is temporary, but what is unseen is eternal.

Medora faced life as the mother of a five-year-old boy, a nine-month-old girl and was pregnant with her fourth child, while desperately missing her second.

On October 8, 1954, Medora gave birth to a second girl, Faith Medora Potter. Medora's physical and mental condition seemed to be getting worse. Several tests were done, both during and after pregnancy. In January of 1955, Wes heard the terrible news that the problem with Medora was much more serious than a mental breakdown, but something fatal, a brain tumor that would only give her about two or three months to live. Once again, relatives and friends began assistance and continued in their prayers.[27]

Facing a terminal illness is one of the most difficult situations, especially for a young mother with three small children, and in Medora's case, especially trying because she had lost Vernon just one year earlier. It would appear that Medora was undergoing similar pain as her Aunt Ellen Whitlock had to endure with more than one tragedy in a short period of time (Chapter 6).

As a student of God's word, Medora certainly turned to the book she knew so well and found comfort for herself and instructions on ways to comfort her oldest son David (see below).

Philippians 1:19, 20. Yes, I will continue to rejoice, for I know that through your prayers and the help given by the Spirit of Jesus Christ, what has happened to me will turn out for my deliverance. I eagerly expect and hope that I will in no way be ashamed, but will have sufficient courage so that now as always Christ will be exalted in my body, whether by life or by death.

Medora began a series of surgeries and radiation treatments that kept her alive for six more years. The surgeries disfigured her head, and the cancer made it increasingly more difficult to walk and speak. Her physical strength began to fail, and her mental faculties declined so much that she was "weak and unable to fulfill normal adult responsibilities." She was not able to be a responsible mother as the effects of the tumor increased.[28]

Grandmother Grace Whitlock came to live and take care of the children for long stretches at a time. Faith, Medora's youngest child, spent most of her early years living with a local family and only has two memories of her mother. Faith remembers a day when she was at home with her mother when Medora started using a walker. She remembers her trying out the walker by walking back and forth across the living room. The second memory is much more important to Faith. At special meetings at the church, Faith remembers accepting Christ as her personal Savior. How special it was when Medora was the one who later talked with Faith, "sharing verses of Scripture and praying with her as she accepted God's free gift of salvation." David remembers that when his mother could no longer read, she still observed her devotional time. She would lie on her bed with her Bible in front of her.[29]

> Isaiah 26:3, 4. You will keep in perfect peace him whose mind is steadfast, because he trusts in you. Trust in the Lord forever, for the Lord, the Lord, is the Rock eternal.

"Medora played the accordion. I can barely remember hearing her play. Mostly the instrument sat in the basement where the bellows eventually rotted."[30]

Grace, Medora's oldest daughter, remembers that Medora's limitations became a normal part of life. There are very few memories of her mother cooking and serving meals, supervision, settling sibling disputes. She began faltering in her steps, fell frequently and had difficulty finding words to say or would have trouble completing sentences. She did attend church with the family when she could, but could not take part in any activities, certainly those expected of a pastor's wife. During the last year of her life, she rarely left the house unless it was a stay in the hospital. Yet

David, her oldest child, remembers only a few times in her treatment and surgeries over six years that he observed Medora to appear frustrated.[31]

Grace, who was just nine months old when Vernon was killed, observed that when she was growing up, her father used to take Medora and the three children in the summer back to the Five Mile to stay with relatives while he continued his pastoral responsibilities in Illinois. On these trips, especially when Medora was still able to travel, pictures that were taken indicated the cruelty of cancer on such a loving mother and the loving care of grandmother, Grace Whitlock.

Grandma Whitlock was the chief connection to Medora for the children. Grandmother read to the children from the Bible as well as story books, taught them to write their names, recognize letters and numbers, and to tie their shoes.[32] Being a woman of prayer and having taught her own daughters the scriptures, Grace was an excellent example of a godly woman to her two granddaughters, Grace and Faith. What seems to be really essential in the spiritual life of children and grandchildren is the ability of a grandparent to show Christ's love in their interactions. I am reminded of St. Paul's letter to Timothy in which he relates how much respect he had for Timothy's sincere faith which Paul had seen in Timothy's mother, Eunice, and grandmother, Lois (II Timothy 1:5). I remember Grace Whitlock to be a soft spoken woman who loved the Lord and showed this love through her caring for us grandchildren. Based on how she brought up my mother and my aunt Alma (Chapter 8), there were never any misunderstandings between parents and grandmother. In addition, Grace and Wesley Potter had many conversations on how best to move forward as Medora's health continued to decline.

Wes and his mother-in-law, Grace Whitlock, had several correspondences in which Grace thought that the treatments should end since Medora's health and well being were in decline, and the children were without a constantly present mother. This gave Wes the "permission" of the relatives to end the treatments.[33]

Medora died late Thursday night, June 15, 1961, at Lakeview Hospital, Danville, Illinois. A funeral service was held at the First Baptist Church, Danville on Saturday, June 17, 1961. Medora's body was transferred to the Halwig Funeral Home in Olean, New York. Wes took the children to the funeral home the day before the funeral but did not take the girls to the funeral itself.[34]

So the spirit of the youngest Whitlock sister, Medora Arvilla Whitlock Potter, went to rest in God's hands, too early for the rest of us. She joined her son, Vernon, waited for her mother Grace, sisters Viola and Alma (Chapters 7-9), and for all of us.

"And Lord, haste the day when the faith shall be sight,
The clouds be rolled back as a scroll,
The trump shall resound and the Lord shall descend,
Even so—it is well with my soul."[35]

"When clothed in His brightness, transported I rise To meet Him in clouds of the sky, His perfect salvation, His wonderful love, I'll shout with the millions on high."[36]

About the time she graduated from high school, Medora wrote a short essay entitled "The Resurrection of Christ." The last paragraph reads:

"How can we, born again believers, think it a thing incredible for us to have victory in our own lives in view of the Power of the Risen Christ within us. Perhaps you do not doubt the possibility of victory in the Christian life, but perhaps there are some who are not Christians, simply because they cannot see how it is possible to live a Christian life. Is that same Power of Deity, that same unfailing purpose which has brought into our lives (those of us who are Christians) the assurance of eternal life, that can give us victory. Cannot this same power of the resurrected Christ make our lives the very manifestation of that resurrected power? Certainly He is the same today. Let us, in remembrance of His mighty victory over the grave, let Him make that victory ours every day that we live. "Yes, we are more than conquerors through Him who loved us."[37]

I am sure that Medora, the other five saints included in this book, and its author would join the Apostle Paul in wishing:

> Ephesians 3:17-19. And I pray that you, being rooted and established in love, may have power, **together with all the saints**, to grasp how wide and long and high and deep is the love of Christ, and to know this love that surpasses knowledge—that you may be filled to the measure of all the fullness of God.

AFTERWORD

During the fall of 2016, as I was writing the final chapters of this book, I placed a CD in my car which I listened to either on trips or when waiting for long stoplights along Route 501 near Coastal Carolina University. The disc, *How Sweet the Sound, My All-Time Favorites* sung by George Beverly Shea, contained a short song written by Della Warren entitled "Jesus Whispers Peace."[1] The song quickly became my favorite because of the lyrics and the knowledge that all of the saints of Allegany may have sung the song, with the exception of my great, great grandmother, Eliza Trowbridge Whitlock, who died before the song was written.

Mr. Shea's introduction to the song, which always touches my heart, is as follows: One of Mr. Shea's friends told him a true story that happened to him during World War II. This friend was severly wounded and lying on the battlefield, drifting in and out of consciousness, when his mother's favorite hymn came to mind. During a period of consciousness, the soldier struggled to sing the hymn. A German soldier approached with drawn bayonet to make sure the American was dead. He bent over and listened to the singing. In words the American could understand, the German said "Sing it again, sing it again." The song apparently touched the German soldier's heart. He did not bayonet the American and he walked off, saving the American's life. With my own mother and the other saints in this book in mind, I began to learn the words to the song.

On Christmas day, 2016, I was taken to the hospital in serious condition, suffering from viral pneumonia and sepsis. While fighting for my life and on a ventilator, I woke from unconsciousness in the middle of the night, all alone in the hospital room. The Great Comforter, the Holy

Spirit, reminded me of the song, and I remember struggling to hum a few lines of the melody and, for certain, the title: "Jesus Whispers Peace."

> There is a name to me most dear, Like sweetest music to my ear,
> For when my heart is troubled, filled with fear, Jesus whispers peace.
> When grief seems more than I can bear, My soul weighed down with heavy care
> And I am sorely tempted to despair, Jesus whispers peace.
> O that the world might hear Him speak the words of comfort that men seek,
> To all the lowly and to the meek, Jesus, he whispers peace.

The words of the song also came to me through the efforts of my wife, Betty, during this time. Her 97-year old mother fell and broke her hip and was in the same hospital. Weighed down with the desire to be with both her husband and her mother, she tirelessly traversed the floors of the hospital to see us both and brought into our rooms Jesus' words of peace.

One month later I was back in the hospital after a blood clot in my right leg made its way through my heart and into my right lung. I certainly remember "Jesus Whispers Peace."

Sometimes the Lord allows problems in our lives that result in having to slow our busy lives and to show us that we can't make it on our own. We then feel broken and are humbled and are ready to hear and respond to his voice. I am sure that the farmers' daughters, described in this book, as the Six Saints from Allegany, in their time of tragedy and loss, would have sung this song, "Broken to Bless."

> You can't put a saddle on a wild stallion.
> He has to be broken before you can ride.
> You can't hurry wisdom or understanding.
> They both come with heartaches and take their sweet time.
> I could drown in my sorrows when the tears come in waves
> Or use them to help someone else find their way.
> We don't learn humility from our success

The failures we go through teach us the most.
I could put on a brave face, act like I'm in control
Or point to the one who I trust with my soul.
The prideful heart demands first place,
the humble heart leaves room for grace.
Because I've been broken, how deeply I can bless
Compassion's been forged in the fires of duress.
As Jesus did for me, How could I do any less?
I've been broken, broken to bless.[2]

As mentioned earlier, God calls His saints to serve. So let us, who have given our lives to the guidance of Jesus Christ, let poetry be one of the "divers ways" he speaks to us. Remember with me the words of this closing song: "Not Too Far From Here."

Somebody's down to their last dime, somebody's running out of time
Not too far from here.
Somebody's got nowhere else to go, somebody needs a little hope
Not too far from here.
And I may not know their names, but I'm praying just the same
That you'll use me Lord to wipe away a tear, 'Cause somebody's crying
Not too far from here.
Somebody's troubled and confused, somebody's got nothing left to lose
Not too far from here.
Somebody's forgotten how to trust, somebody's dying for love
Not too far from here.
It may be a stranger's face, but I'm praying for your grace
To move in me and take away the fear, 'Cause somebody's hurting
Not too far from here.
Help me Lord not to turn away from pain
Help me not to rest while those around me weep
Give me your strength and compassion
When somebody finds the road of life too steep.

Now I'm letting down my guard and I'm opening my heart
Help me speak your love to every needful ear.
Jesus is waiting
Not too far from here.[3]

Psalms 107:13-15 Then they cried to the Lord in their trouble, and he saved them from their distress. He brought them out of darkness and the deepest gloom and broke away their chains. Let them give thanks to the Lord for his unfailing love and his wonderful deeds for men.

John 6:39, 40 For I have come down from heaven, not to do my will but to do the will of him who sent me. And this is the will of him who sent me, that I should lose none of all that he has given me, but raise them up at the last day. For my Father's will is that everyone who looks to the Son and believes in him shall have eternal life, and I will raise him up at the last day.

Ephesians 3: 20, 21 Now to him who is able to do immeasurably more than all we ask or imagine, according to his power that is at work within us, to him be glory in the church and to Christ Jesus throughout **all generations**, forever and ever! Amen.

Notes

Foreword

1. Henry Alford, *The Works of John Donne with a Memoir of His Life* (London:John W. Parker, 1839). vol V, 110.

Chapter 1.

1. For an explanation of the Big Bang Theory and gravitational waves see: Charles Q. Choi. "Our Expanding Universe: Age, History & Other Facts." Available at: www.space.com/52-the-expanding-universe-from-the-big-bang-to-today.html.
2. C.S. Lewis, "God in Outer Space." *The Joyful Christian* (New York: Macmillan, 1977) 5, 6.
3. Mary A. Lathbury, "Day is Dying in the West," 1877. *Hymns for the Living Faith* (Carol Stream, Illinois:Hope Publishing, 1977) 557, verse 2.
4. Joesph Addison, "The Spacious Firmament on High," 1712. Ibid., 54, verse 1.
5. Viola W. Dunham, *Viola Fern Whitlock Diaries.* August 13, 1973.

Chapter 2.

1. Paul Puglis, *Soil Survey of Cattaraugus County, New York* (Albany: United Staates Department of Agriculture, National Resources Conservation Service, 2007). Available at: http://soildatamart.nrcs.usda/Manuscripts/NYOC.
2. Ibid;, 459, 466, 471-72, 495, 499, 507-08.
3. Ibid., 511-12, 518, 521, 538, 540.
4. Ibid., 551-54.

5. Cyrus McKay, "Town of Allegany," *The History of Cattaraugus County, New York.* Available at: http://www.paintedhills.org/CATTARAGUS/allegany1879Bios/Allegany1879Hist.htm.

Chapter 3.

1. US Census 1810; "John Whitlock Household, Genoa Township" 1810. Series M252, roll 31, p. 80, *National Archives Micropublication Series,* National Archives, Washington, D. C.
2. Census Office 1810.
3. John Swanton, *The Indian Tribes of North America,* Washington, D.C.: Bureau of American Ethnology, Smithsonian Institute, 2003).
4. Jean D. Worden, "Records from the First Presbyterian Church of Ithaca, New York." (*Tompkins County New York Church Records,* 1983) Manuscript no. 4045, Box 27, Cornell Univ. Archives, Ithaca, New York.
5. US Census 1830, 1850.
6. Frank Topping, "Travelling," in *Lord of the Evening* (London: Lutterworth Press, 1979) 68.
7. US Census 1830.
8. US Census 1850
9. Whitney R. Cross, *The Burned-over District: The Social and Intellectual History of Enthusiastic Religion in Western New York, 1800-1850* (Ithaca: Cornell Univ. Press, 1950) 3-6.

Chapter 4.

1. John Calvin, "Institutes of the Christian Religion," 1536. In *Living Selections from the Devotional Classics* (Nashville: The Upper Room, 1958). 5, 6.
2. *Vine's Greek New Testament Dictionary,* 1940. Available at: http://gospelhall.org/bible/bible.php?search=hagios&lang=greek.
3. Charles Wesley, "Love Divine, All Loves Excelling." 1747. In *Hymns for the Living Church,* Ibid. 75.

Chapter 5.

1. US Census, 1850.
2. Ibid.

3. "Population Schedule, Cattaraugus County, New York, June 18, 1870," *National Archives Micropublication Series*. M593, roll 908, p.34.

4. "Organization of the Confederate States of America." *Journal of the Congress of the Confederate States of America I (1861-1865)*. First Session, February 4, March 16, 1861. US Government Printing Office, 1904.

5. Frederick Phisterer, *New York in the War of the Rebellion* (Albany: Weed, Parsons, 1890). 7-10.

6. Valgene Dunham, *Allegany to Appomattox: The Life and Letters of Private William Whitlock of the 188th New York Volunteers* (Syracuse: Syracuse Univ. Press, 2013). 15, 16; Mark H. Dunkelman, *Brothers One and All: Espirit de Corps in a Civil War Regiment* (Baton Rouge: Louisiana State Univ. Press, 2004), 33; Mark H. Dunkelman, "Amos Humiston: Union soldier who died at the Battle of Gettysburg." Posted August 19, 1997. Available at: www.historynet.com/amos-humiston-who-died-at-the-battle-of-gettysburg.htm.

7. For William Whitlock's war experiences, see Dunham, 2013. The book includes the transcriptions of the Whitlock Papers by Bill Potter. Private Whitlock was killed on February 6, 1865 in the Battle of Hatcher's Run II. Whitney Collection.

8. William Whitlock to Mary Eliza Trowbridge Whitlock, February 3, 1865. This is the last letter William wrote to his wife, Lide, before he was killed in battle on February 6, 1865 at the Battle of Hatcher's Run II. Available in Dunham, Ibid., 145, 146.

9. Alanson Jones to Morris Whitlock, March 14, 1865. This letter is from a tent mate of William Whitlock to his brother concerning William's death. Letter #40, Whitlock Collection. Dunham, Ibid., 167-9.

10. William O. Cushing, "Under His Wings I am Safely Abiding," 1896. In *Hymns for the Living Church*, Ibid., 310.

11. Jessie Adams, "I Feel the Winds of God Today," 1907. In *Hymns for the Living Church, Ibid.*, 449.

12. Henry W. Baker, "The King of Love My Shepherd Is," 1868. In *Hymns for the Living Church*, Ibid., 46.

Chapter 6.

1. Isaac Watts, "O God, Our Help in Ages Past," 1719. In *Hymns for the Living Church*, Ibid., 48.

2. Valgene Dunham, 2013, Ibid. Appendix A, 189-90.

3. William Whitlock, Whitlock Letters, 1864, 1865. Whitney Collection, Howard Mark Whitney, Allegany, New York; Valgene Dunham, Ibid., 8, Appendix C.

4. *Population Schedule, Cattaraugus County, New York*, June 18, 1879, M593, roll 908, p. 14, *National Archives Micropublication Series*; "Minutes of School District #5, Town of Allegany," Whitney Collection; Vernon E. Field, *Five Mile Farms and Farmers*, revised and published by James Hitchcock, date unknown, Dunham Collection.

5. Ibid.

6. Valgene Dunham, *Echoes From the Empty House on the Corner: Family, Faith and Tragedy*, self published. 2016. 28.

7. Viola W. Dunham, *Viola Fern Whitlock Dunham Diaries*, November 4, 1973.

8. Valgene Dunham, Ibid., 28-31.

9. Ibid.

10. David Watson, *Called & Committed: World Changing Discipleship* (Wheaton, Illinois: Harold Shaw, 1982) 42.

11. Valgene Dunham, Ibid., 28.

12. Viola Whitlock Dunham, VWD Diary, 1973; Valgene Dunham, Ibid., 30.

13. Sabrina Beasley McDonald, "Finding Comfort in the Midst of Grief," *Family Life*. Available at: www.familylife.com/articles/topics/marriages/challenges/death-of-spouse/finding-comfort-in-the-midst-of-grief

14. Dunham, Ibid., 29-31.

15. "Hinsdale Man." *Olean Times Herald*, January 10, 16, 1945.

16. "Alumni News." Lenna Whitlock, *Wheaton College Yearbook*, March, 1955.

17. Dunham, Ibid., 31. Allegany, New York Cemetery, Available at: http://www.rootsweb.ancestry.com~nycattr/cemetery/allegany/index.htm.

18. Georg Neumark, "If Thou but Suffer God to Guide Thee," 1641. In *Hymns of the Living Church*, Ibid., 420.

Chapter 7.

1. Valgene Dunham, Ibid., 76. 77.

2. Ibid., 67.

3. Ibid., 77.

4. Ibid., 32.

5. Ibid., 87. Dunham, *Allegany to Appomattox*, Ibid., 190.

6. Ibid., 133. Dunham, *Allegany to Appomattox*, Ibid., 190.

7. Ibid., 169. Dunham, *Allegany to Appomattox*, Ibid., 190.

8. Dunham, *Allegany to Appomattox*, Ibid., 181.

9. John Wesley, "Happiness," March 29, 1737. Ed. Paul Lambourne Higgins. In *Living Selections from the Devotional Classics* (Nashville; The Upper Room, 1967). 26.

10. Clare Earl Whitlock, *Diaries*, January 2, 1932; Ibid., June 5, 20, 23, 26.

11. Ellen Banks Elwell, "Heart." *Devotions for Moms* (Wheaton, Illinois: Tyndale House, 2005). p. Heart.

12. Personal communications, Nancy Billings Chesebro, Grace Potter Albright, 2015.

13. Ellen Banks Elwell, "Humility." *Devotions for Moms,* Ibid.

Chapter 8.

1. *Olean Times Herald*, March 16, 1914.

2. "Physicians' Visiting List," Author unknown, 1914. Dunham Collection.

3. Vernon E. Field. Ibid.

4. *Olean Times Herald*, August 15, 1919. "Annual Reunion of Whitlock-Trowbridge Families at the Five Mile," 14; Ibid., August 14, 1925, "Allegany," p. 11.

5. R. R. Hess. "Five Mile Baptist Church," *Olean Times Herald*, July 14, 1928, 2.

6. *Olean Times Herald*, June 24, 1931; "Allegany Has Graduation On Tuesday," p. 3; Ibid., September 11, 1931. "Allegany," p. 7.

7. Jean Weaver, "Work in Missionaries, Fields of Endeavor Intrigue Pastor's Wife," *Lorain Journal*, September 13, 1952.

8. Marriage Certification, Rushford, New York, May 7, 1932, Witnesses: Kenneth Chesebro, Alma Whitlock. Appendix C. Valgene Dunham, *Echoes from the Empty House on the Corner: Family, Faith, and Tragedy*, Ibid., 229.

9. A. H. Blaisdell to Verne L. Dunham, April 23, 1934. Dunham Collection.

10. Viola Whitlock Dunham, Diaries, December 7, 1973.

11. Dunham, Ibid., Chapter 6. Appendix M, p 241; Appendix N, p. 244-248.

12. Lloyd John Ogilvie, *When God First Thought of You* (Waco, Texas: Word Books, 1978). 67.

13. Viola Whitlock Dunham, *Diaries*, 1971. December 12, 14, 15. Dunham Collection.

14. Viola Whitlock Dunham, Ibid., October 21, 1972.

15. Mary Blagg, "He Came, Stayed, and Paid the Price," *State News*, Dover, Delaware, November 13, 1972, p. 19.

16. Viola Whitlock Dunham, Ibid., January 5, 10, 11. 1973.

17. Ibid., August 3, September 16-19, 1974.

18. Ibid., March 8-10, 13, 20, 27, April 1-8, May 8, July 2, 4, July 12, 21, August, 17,18, September 11, 17, 20, December 19, 22, 24, 1989.

19. Ibid.

20. Ibid.

21. Using six letters from 1998, two from 1999, and one from 2000, all written to Frank and Vaughn Dunham Estep, I examined the letters for misspellings, repetition, stress levels as indicated by capitalization and underlining, and child-like descriptions of her daily existence. In a letter Viola wrote on November 16, 1988, she described the renovations going on at Eden Heights. "Many improvement happening here every day—carpenters, tile floor layers—paper hangers—a new division for Elshymer (still don't know the spelling—so I'm going to my Dictionary—Alzheimers Disease—a degenerative disease of the central nervous system characterized by premature senile mental deterioration—I may be on the way!"

22. Carrie E. Breck, "Face to Face with Christ My Savior," 1898. In *Hymns for the Living Church*, Ibid., 534.

23. William W. How, "For All the Saints," 1864. In *Hymns for the Living Church*, Ibid., 533.

Chapter 9. Alma Maud Whitlock Chesebro Rex

1. A. A. Milne, *Winnie the Pooh*. 1926.

2. Nate Robinson, New Orleans Pelicans, National Basketball Association.

3. "Colic cures," *Earthclinic*, Available at: http://www.earthclinic.com/cures/colic/html.

4. Stephen and Nancy Chesebro, personal communication, 2015.

5. "Physicians' Visiting List," Ibid. Dunham Collection.

6. Claire Earl Whitlock, *Diaries*, December 27, 1932.

7. Emily L. Shirreff. "Gracious Savior, Who Didst Honor," 1814-1897. In *Hymns for the Living Church*, Ibid., 530.

8. Henry Ware, Jr., "Happy the Home When God is There," 1846. Ibid., 531.

9. See Viola Whitlock Dunham's *Diaries*, 1973, 1988, 1995.

10. Clare Earl Whitlock, *Diaries*, Ibid.

11. Folliott S. Pierpoint, "For the Beauty of the Earth," 1864. In *Hymns for the Living Church*, Ibid.,

12. *Olean Times Herald*, July 14, 1928, p. 2.

13. Clare Earl Whitlock, *Diaries*, Ibid., June 26, 1934.

14. Ibid., August 18.

15. "Bert Chesebro Family Linage." Chesebro Collection. Stephen and Nancy Chesbro, Murrells Inlet, South Carolina.

16. Clare Earl Whitlock, Ibid., February 10, 22, 1934; February 22, 1935.

17. Ibid., March 4-8, August 23, 1935.

18. Ibid., November 6, 13; December 24, 1935.

19. Ibid., January 18-20, 22, 26; February 8, 9, 1936.

20. Ibid., February 27; March 12, 13, 21, 22, 1936.

21. Ibid., December 19, 20, 25, 28, 29, 1936.

22. Stephen Chesebro, personal communication, January 2016.

23. Ibid.

24. Stephen and Nancy Chesebro, personal communication, January 2016.

25. Horatio G. Spafford, "When Peace Like a River Attendeth," 1873. In *Hymns for the Living Church*, Ibid., 401.

26. Stephen and Nancy Chesebro, Ibid.

27. Ibid. David Potter, personal communication, 2015.

28. Stephen and Nancy Chesebro, Ibid.

29. Viola Whitlock Dunham, *Diaries*, January 1, 18, 21, 1981.

30. Horatio G. Spafford, Ibid.

31. Viola Whitlock Dunham, Ibid., 1992.

32. Mike Chesebro, "A Gift of Heart," Grade 5. November 30, 1983.

33. Viola Whitlock Dunham, Ibid., July 4, 5, 16, 20-25, 29, 30, 1993; David Potter, personal communication, 2013.

34. Viola Whitlock Dunham. Letters to Frank and Vaughn Dunham Estep, Dunham Collection.

35. Nancy Chesebro, personal communication, January, 2016.

36. Esther Chesebro Smith, obituary. *Reporter-Times.com/MD-Times.com*. 2008; Sephen Chesebro, personal communication, January, 2016.

37. *Olean Times Herald*, December, 2008. "Alma M. Whitlock Rex (1917-2008)."

38. Frank Topping, "Bedtime," *Lord of the Evening* (Lutterworth Press (London, 1979) 13.

39. Carolina Sandell Berg, "Children of the Heavenly Father," In *Hymns for the Living Church*, Ibid., 41.

Chapter 10. Medora Arvilla Whitlock Potter

1. *The Olean Evening Herald*, Wednesday, April 23, 1922.
2. David Robert Potter, personal communication, October 28, 2013.
3. Grace Potter Albright, personal communication, October 27, 2013.
4. David Robert Potter, Ibid.
5. Christian Burke, "Lord of Life and King of Glory," In *Hymns for the Living Church*, Ibid., 528.
6. David Robert Potter, Ibid.
7. Medora Arvilla Whitlock Potter, *Diary*, 1943, January 5, 9, 14, 15, 25.
8. Clare Earl Whitlock *Diaries*, Ibid., August 1, 1935.
9. Christian Burke, Ibid.
10. *Olean Times Herald*, June 22, 1940, p. 5; "Allegany High School Commencement Exercises, Class of 1940." Potter and Whitney Collections.
11. Potter Collection.
12. Medora Arvilla Whitlock, *Diary*, 1943. January 2, 9, 13, 22, 26; February 22; March 1, 5, 12, 31; April 10, 21, 24, 30; May 14, 17.
13. Faith Potter White, personal communication, 2013.
14. *Olean Times Herald*, July 3, 1948, p. 3; "Wesley Potter Obituary," Casey, Halwig, Harle (funeral home).
15. Ibid.
16. Davis College, Available at: http://www.davisny.edu/about/history-of-davis/past-presidents. *Practical Bible Training School Report*, John A. Davis Memorial Bible School, Inc., Bible School Park, New York. Report Card, report for Whitlock, Medora, for the year 1945-46, ending May 28, 1946. Potter and Whitney Collections.
17. *Olean Times Herald*, July 3, 1948. "Wesley Potter, Wed;" Mrs. John Robinson, Correspondent, *Lima Recorder*, Lima, New York, April 8, 1948.
18. *Olean Times Herald*, Ibid.; Grace Potter Albright, personal communication, 2013.
19. David Potter, Grace Potter Albright, Faith Potter White, Cecil Pennington Potter, personal communications, 2013-2016.
20. David Potter, personal communication, January 17, 2014.
21. Cecile Pennington Potter, personal communication, April 7, 2013. David Potter, Ibid.
22. Faith Potter White, personal communication, January, 2014. Cecile Pennington Potter, Ibid.

23. David Potter, Grace Albright, Faith White and Cecile Potter, personal communications, 2914-2016.

24. David Potter, personal communication, 2015.

25. Frank E. Graeff, "Does Jesus Care?" 1901. In *Hymns for the Living Church*, Ibid., 416.

26. David Potter, Ibid.

27. David Potter, Grace Albright, Faith White, Cecile Potter, Ibid, 2014-2016.

28. David Potter, Grace Albright, Faith White, Ibid., 2014-2016.

29. Faith Potter White, David Potter, personal communications, Ibid.

30. Ibid.

31. Grace Potter Albright, David Potter, personal communications, Ibid.

32. Grace Potter Albright, personal communication, 2013. .

33. David Potter, Ibid.

34. Grace Potter Albright, David Potter, Ibid., 2016

35. Horatio G. Spafford, Ibid. In *Hymns for the Living Church*, 401.

36. Fanny Crosby, "A Wonderful Savior Is Jesus My Lord," 1890. In *Hymns for the Living Church*, Ibid., 402.

37. Medora Orvilla Whitlock Potter, Potter Collection.

Afterword

1.   Della Warren, "Jesus Whispers Peace," Word Music, Inc., Rodeheaver Co. 1936. Rodeheaver, Hall Mack Co., 1938. Print licensed to author from Warner/Chappell Music, Inc.

2.   Steve Siler, "Broken to Bless," Silerland Music, Music for the Soul. Administered by Clear Box Rights, ASCAP. Lyrics courtesy of "Musicforthesoul.org."

3.   Ty Lacy and Steve Siler, "Not too Far from Here," Lyrics courtesy of "Musicforthesoul.org." Shepherd's Fold Music; Ariose Music Group.

Ancestry of the Six Saints*

William Whitlock x <u>Mary Eliza Trowbridge</u> (1831-1889)
↓
Euzetta, Stanley, Clara, Henry
      Stanley Mead Whitlock x Medora Linderman
          ↓
      Ray, Clare, Bessie
      Ray John Whitlock x <u>Ellen Jane Linderman</u> (1884 -1962)
      Clare Earl Whitlock x <u>Grace Olivia Whitney Whitlock</u> (1891-1970)
          ↓
          <u>Viola Fern Whitlock Dunham</u> (1914-2005)
          <u>Alma Maud Whitlock Chesebro Rex</u> (1917-2008)
          <u>Medora Arvilla Whitlock Potter</u> (1922-1961)

    *Six Saints are underlined.

References

General
> Hymns; *Hymns for the Living Church*, Carol Stream, Illinois: Hope Publishing, 1974.
> Scripture: The Scofield Study Bible, *New International Version*. New York: Oxford Univ. Press, 2004.

Adams, William. 1893. Ed. *Historical Gazetteer and Biographical Memorial of Cattauragus County, New York*. Syracuse: Lyman and Horton.

Ahlstrom, Sydney. 1972. *A Religious History of the American People*. New Haven: Yale Univ. Press.

Alford, Henry. 1839. *The Works of John Donne: with a memoir of his life*. London: John W. Parker.

Calvin, John. 1536. "Institutes of the Christian Religion". Ed. Norman Victor Hope, 1958. *Living Selections from the Devotional Classics*. Nashville: The Upper Room.

Channing, Steven. 1974. *Crisis of Fear: Secession in South Carolina*. New York: W.W. Norton.

Cross, Whitney. 1950. *The Burned-Out District: The Social and Intellectual History of Enthusiastic Religion in Western New York*. Ithaca: Cornell Univ. Press.

Deschesne, David. 2011. "The Attributes of a Saint." *Fort Fairfield Journal*, January 12.

Available at: http://www.fortfairfieldjournal.com/mpl_saint.htm.

Dunham, Valgene L. 2013. *Allegany to Appomattox: The Life and Letters of Private William Whitlock of the 188ᵗʰ New York Volunteers.* Syracuse: Syracuse Univ. Press.

_____. 2016. *Echoes from the Empty House on the Corner: Family, Faith and Tragedy.* Self published.

_____. 2016. *Gregory's New York Brigade: Blue-Collar Reserves in Dusty Blue Jackets.* Bloomington, Indiana: Archway.

Dunham, Viola Whitlock. *Diaries*, August 13, 1973. Original author unknown. Dunham Collection.

Dunkelman, Mark H. 2004. *Brothers One and All: Espirit de Corps in a Civil War Regiment.* Baton Rouge: Louisiana State Univ. Press.

Edwards, Elizabeth. 2009. *Resilience:The New Afterword.* New York: Random.

Ellis, Franklin. [1879] 2004. "Town of Ischua." Transcribed by Joanne Donk, In *The History of Cattaraugus County, New York.* USGenWeb Project. Available at:

http://www.rootsweb.ancestry.com/~nycattar/1879history/ischua.htm.

Gaustad, Edwin and Leigh Schmidt. 2002. *The Religious History of America.* Revised edition. San Francisco: HarperCollins.

Hampton, David. 2005. *Methodism: Empire of the Spirit.* New Haven: Yale Univ. Press.

Haynali, Carolyn. 2013. "Alzheimer's Patient's Prayer." *Alzheimers net.* Available at:

www.alzheimers.net/2013-08-20/poem-alzheimers-patients-prayer/

Krippayne, Scott and Steve Siler. 1998. "More Like a Whisper." *The Martins. Dream Big.* Nashville: Spring Hill Music Group.

Lacy, Ty and Steve Siler. 1994. "Not Too Far from Here." Shepherd's Fold, BMI/Aroise, ASCAP, Capitol CMG Publishing.

Leonard, Bill. 2005. *Baptists in America.* Columbia Contemporary American Religion Series. New York: Columbia Univ. Press.

Lewis, C.S. 1967. *Christian Reflections.* Grand Rapids: W.B. Eerdmans.

Lucado, Max. 2007. *3:16: The Numbers of Hope.* Nashville: Thomas Nelson.

MacAdam, Barbara D. 2017. "My Sister, My Friend." *Best Poems Encyclopedia.* Available at:

http://100.best-poems.net/my-sister-my-friend.html.

MacDonald, Sabrina. 2016. "Finding Comfort in the Midst of Grief." *Family Life.* Available at: www.familylife.com/articles/topics/marriages/challenges/death-of-spouse/finding-comfort-in-the-midst-of-grief.

McKay, Cyrus. 1879. "Town of Allegany," *The History of Cattaraugus County, New York.* Transcribed by Samantha Eastman, 2004. Available at:

http://www.paintedhills.org/CATTARAGUS/allegany1879 Bios/Allegany1879Hist,htm.

Ogilvie, lloyd, John. 1978. *When God First Thought of You.* Waco: Word Books.

Olean Evening Herald, August 23, 1922.

"Physicians' Visiting List," 1914. Author unknown. Dunham Collection.

"Population Schedule, Cattaraugus County, New York., June 18, 1870," M593, roll 908. *National Archives Micropublication Series.*

"Prayer for My Sister." 2017. Unknown author. Available at: *Prayer for Anxiety.* http://prayerforanxiety.com/2016/07/06/prayer-for-my-sister.

Puglia, Paul. 2007. *Soil Survey of Cattaraugus County, New York.* Albany: United States Department of Agriculture, National Resources Conservation Service.

Siler, Steve. 2015. "Broken to Bless." *Music for the Soul.* Silerland Music.

Swanton, John. 2003. *The Indian Tribes of North America.* Washington Bulletin, Washington,D.C: Bureau of American Ethnology, Smithsonian Institute.

Topping, Frank. 1979. "Travelling," verse 3. In *Lord of the Evening.* London: Lutterworth.

_____ 1979. "Bedtime," verse 4. Ibid.

U.S. Census 1810; "John Whitlock Household, Genoa Township." Series M252, roll 31. *National Archives Micropublication Series,* Washington, D.C.

"U.S. Census 1830, 1850, 1855, 1860." National Archives, Washington, D.C.

Vine's Greek New Testament Dictionary. Available at:

http://gospelhall.org/bible/bible.php?search=hagios&lang=greek.

Warren, Della. 1936. "Jesus Whispers Peace." *How Sweet the Sound, My All-Time Favorites*, George Beverly Shea. World Music, Inc.

Watson, David. 1982. *Called & Committed: World-Changing Discipleship.* Wheaton, Illinois: Harold Shaw.

Wesley, John. 1737. "Happiness." Selections from the Journal of John Wesley, ed. Paul L. Higgins. *Great Devotional Classics.* Nashville: The Upper Room, 1967.

Whitlock, Clare. *Clare Whitlock Diaries.* Dunham Collection, Valgene L. Dunham, Conway, South Carolina.

Whitlock, William. 1864, 1865. *Whitlock Letters.* Whitney Collection, Howard Mark Whitney, Conway, South Carolina,

Worden, Jane D. 1983. "Records from the First Presbyterian Church of Ithaca, New York," *Tompkins County New York Church Records*, Manuscript no. 4045, Box 27, Cornell Univ. Archives, Ithaca, New York.

INDEX

Printed in the United States
By Bookmasters